Burle Marx

Roberto Burle Marx is a musician whose accents are perceived through another sense: light. LÚCIO COSTA

Marta Iris Montero

Translated by Ann Wright

Burle Marx

The Lyrical Landscape

Foreword by Martha Schwartz

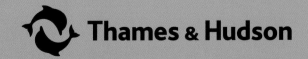
Thames & Hudson

First published in the United Kingdom in 2001 by
Thames & Hudson Ltd, 181A High Holborn,
London WC1V 7QX

© 1997 and 2001 Marta Iris Montero
Translated from the Spanish by Ann Wright
English translation © 2001 Thames & Hudson Ltd, London
Foreword © 2001 Martha Schwartz

British Library Cataloguing-in-Publication Data
A catalogue record for this book is available from
the British Library

ISBN 0-500-51046-6

Original design concept by Juan Cavallero
Picture research by Lucía Cedrón

Printed and bound in Hong Kong by C & C Offset

[Above left] Rio Business Centre (photo Roland Paiva)

[Above right] Santo Antônio da Bica
(photo Nelson Rivera Monteiro)

Contents

Acknowledgments

It was a smiling garden;
it was a tranquil crystal source;
from a bush at its edge,
appeared an immaculate rose.

SERAFÍN AND JOAQUÍN
ALVAREZ QUINTERO

To my mother, Haydée Iris, who made this book possible, and to the gardens of my grandmother, Angelita, which made such an impression on my childhood.

I would also like to thank many colleagues and friends for all their help and support. Special thanks to the photographer Roland Paiva, who accompanied me with his cameras on magical expeditions; the architect Juan Di Filippo who acted as guide; the designer Juan Carlos Cavallero, who had to design the layouts of the Spanish edition twice; the writer Miguel Briante, who revised the first draft in Spanish; Ruth Blum, architect and planner, who gave advice and support throughout the preparation of the English edition; and my daughter, Lucía Cedrón, for being my collaborator in this project when she was only fifteen.

6

Foreword

When I think about Burle Marx, I am struck by sheer gratitude for his existence. As I have always felt a bit of an outsider to the landscape architecture profession, I am forever searching for those kindred spirits who might guide my own exploration and give me faith that my own direction might be of use and bear fruit.

Burle Marx has always been and will remain for me a shining light in the somewhat dim universe of landscape art and architecture. Like my other hero and model, Isamu Noguchi, the strength of Burle Marx's work is that it is a direct expression of his spirit. Burle Marx's bold use of form and colour, combined with his painterly approach, express the force of his personality and sensibility, which, to me, is the necessary core to all art. This force, his art, transmits and connects to everyone around him.

A great artist in whose mind and heart were no boundaries, Burle Marx was a fluid thinker unconcerned by living within limits. Whether designing a landscape or painting, eating, playing music or throwing a great party, he lived and created wholeheartedly and with gusto. And because his life was as creative as his gardens, he showed us that it is just as important to invent *what* to do with one's life as *how* to live it.

Burle Marx was not only a prominent landscape architect with an international reputation. In Brazil he was a national hero. Through his passion for the native landscape and his artistic skill in depicting this love, he helped an entire nation define itself. In his fascination with natural processes, with the artifacts of nature that he lovingly collected and nurtured, and the love of our human (and in particular, Brazilian) nature,

he balanced humanism with naturalism. I find his connection to his culture as significant as his enthusiasm for his native landscape, and it is precisely this essential connection between humans and their environments that he expressed and celebrated in his work.

Through understanding the great range of Burle Marx's works, interests and the influences on him, we professionals should take heart that it is possible to integrate art and science and to believe that it is only with our personal intuition, spirit and sensibilities that we can bring meaning and form to our environment, wherever that may be.

Martha Schwartz

Introduction

The bulldozers arrived and demolished what was left of the Plaza República del Perú, the only public garden in Argentina by the Brazilian landscape designer Roberto Burle Marx. Although for me it was a catastrophe, it made me all the more determined to publish this book. The text is based on the thesis I wrote for my diploma at the French National School of Landscaping in Versailles, housed in what used to be the Potager du Roi, Louis XIV's orchard. After the square was demolished, the Argentine Architectural Association referred to 'the Burle Marx ruins' and I decided I had to tell my compatriots that beneath those ruins lay treasure.

I met Roberto Burle Marx in 1971 when, as adviser on urban design to the Mayor of Buenos Aires, my opinion was sought on the landscaping layouts he proposed as part of a contract from the municipality to regenerate the Barrio Sur.[1] This ambitious project did not go ahead because a loan from the Inter-American Development Bank was not forthcoming. Yet I was determined that Buenos Aires should have at least one design by the Brazilian artist. I put the idea to Mayor Saturnino Montero Ruiz, my father, whose slogan was 'free space, green space' and who had just bought some land between Salguero Street and Figueroa Alcorta Avenue to make a public space. It was to be called the Plaza República del Perú because Peru had offered a sculpture of the Inca Garcilaso by the sculptor Roca Rey, to commemorate the 150th anniversary of its independence. I suggested that Burle Marx carry out the design. The Mayor accepted on condition that he donated his services. Burle Marx and his two partners, Haruyoshi Ono and José Tabacow, duly donated their work and the Plaza República del Perú was born. I was given the task of coordinating the project.

This was my first experience of working with Burle Marx. Later, when I was a widow in exile in Paris and determined not to return to the country that had caused me so much pain, I wrote telling him my story and asking for advice on where to study landscape architecture. He answered very affectionately and said he would be coming to Paris to accept the Gold Medal of the Academy of Architecture. We resumed our friendship. His visit coincided with an international competition for a park in La Villette. Burle Marx put me in touch with some of his disciples who were entering the competition and I joined a Brazilian team which obtained a mention.

Five years later I went to Rio de Janeiro to work with Burle Marx himself. I accompanied him on his expeditions to different parts of Brazil to collect unknown species of plants, which he then classified and nurtured in his nursery gardens. I joined him in fieldwork and helped him design and construct gardens. We worked together again, this time as partners, on a project for one of the terraces of the Pompidou Centre in Paris. I visited him every year around his birthday, 4 August, which he celebrated with memorable parties in his house 60 kilometres outside Rio, surrounded by friends from all over the world. Our relationship continued until his death in 1994.

When he had come to Buenos Aires to design the Plaza Perú Burle Marx was sixty-two years old, with a luminous white head of hair and enormous vitality. We had liked each other immediately. His method was to work with the local flora, and he had spent weeks studying our autochthonous plants. We had gone on trips to places where the original vegetation still existed because, in Buenos Aires at that time, plants were mostly imported from abroad. Fortunately there was still primitive forest in parts of the province of Buenos Aires and he had examined, identified and selected his repertoire of plants for the square from there.

When the time had come for planting, however, the municipal nurseries did not have the species Burle Marx had planned. I had to transplant mature tipu, jacaranda and coral trees from other squares. Over the years, the coral trees dried out from lack of water. They were replaced by very slow-growing trumpet trees, so that in the short term the Plaza Perú did not have enough shade. The interplay between the colours of the foliage and flowers he had grouped together never materialized. The mineral elements he chose for the plaza – grey paving stones and ochre-coloured cement – faded with time. The ingenious mural painted on the wall of the adjacent house disappeared when the building was pulled down. And the spiral – a cement tower with a sandpit on top where children could play in the sun away from the noise of the street – irritated the authorities because its walls were daubed with anti-government slogans.

An invention of which Burle Marx himself was proud, the spiral – baptised in his studio the 'kiddieplay-wall' and successfully reproduced in squares throughout Brazil – received the most criticism. People said it was dangerous for children; that they could fall and hurt themselves; that it seemed specially designed for graffiti; that the sandpit would become contaminated; that the structure as a whole attracted down-and-outs. In 1995, a new mayor found the solution: the bulldozer. As a way of getting rid of undesirables, it seemed to me an inappropriate measure. In Paris, Haussmann demolished medieval houses and created avenues to give the army a better view so they could advance and repress the masses. A flat square is easier to police but it does not solve the problems of drug addicts and homeless people.

This is the chronicle of an unfinished square that became a ruin before it was completed. Yet, amongst the rubble lie hidden riches: the great landscape designer's project still waiting to be realized as it was originally envisaged.

The shame I felt over the demolition of the work (or what was left of it) that Burle Marx had donated to the Argentinian people spurred me finally to publish this book, which had been interrupted by my return to Argentina. Through its pages I would like to share what I learned from him, what he was like, how he worked, how he thought. It is my tribute to the master.

Marta Iris Montero

[left] Floral arrangements for a party, made with *Cordyline* and *Heliconia*. The white flowers are *Clusias*, the red flowers *Alpinia* and the yellow flowers *Stifftia*.

Part One

Landscape of a Life

We were in his study, Roberto sitting in his rocking chair, his impressive figure belying his years, me beside him. He had received a letter from François Burkhardt, Director of the Pompidou Centre in Paris, thanking him for his hospitality during a recent stay in Rio. He decided to reply but, because his sight was by then very poor, he dictated his moving letter to me, in French, off the cuff, with his customary lucidity and without hesitating or correcting a single sentence. In the letter he expressed his existential outlook and the ideas that informed his life and work. It was an illuminating summary:

I have worked a great deal and, at my age, looking back over my life, I feel that Brazil provided me with enormous possibilities. There have been happy moments, successes, and also battles lost. But I always worked with courage and love, searching for the way best suited to my temperament.

In countries that do not have an accepted idiom for talking about art, we have a strange, unconventional way of expressing ourselves. It is frequently the unconscious talking. In Europe, children begin their artistic apprenticeship at their mothers' breasts. In Brazil, where the flora is so rich, we have the chance to explore for ourselves.

I live in a state of continual discovery in response to nature and the people who live on the margins of the world. I don't deny that I owe much to European culture, but I live in *this* world, where experience is linked to instinct and where, even though they haven't heard of Leonardo da Vinci, Piero della Francesca, Rainer Maria Rilke, Roger Martin du Gard or Mallarmé, people feel a strong need to express themselves through art. And that is why I say we live in a land of promise. I hope that the influences that come to me from the Brazilian people will continue to be vividly expressed in my work.

Roberto Burle Marx

Chapter One

The Life of Burle Marx

Cecília Burle.

Wilhelm Marx.

Roberto Burle Marx was born in the city of São Paulo in Brazil on 4 August 1909. His mother, Cecília Burle, came from an old Brazilian family of French and English descent, from the state of Pernambuco. She was a pianist, sang beautifully and had a fine appreciation of nature. His father, Wilhelm Marx, a cultured and adventurous German Jew, arrived in Brazil in 1895. He had been born in Trier, the same city as Karl Marx.

Wilhelm Marx's export business took him to Morocco and the United States before he decided to settle in Recife, in the Brazilian state called 'Northeast'. He reared dogs and horses and loved music. While he was taking piano classes from Cecília and she learning German from him, they fell in love and were married in 1901. They chose São Paulo as their home and, in between trips to Europe and moving house several times, they had six children.

In 1913, they moved to Rio de Janeiro and bought a large house in the district of Leme. Their family included Anna Piascek, a Hungarian woman who lived to the grand age of 102 and whom Burle Marx grew to love like a second mother. Anna and Cecília taught the young Roberto to recognize flowers and to enjoy music. Wilhelm took great pains with his children's education, teaching them the pleasures of literature and languages. As well as Portuguese, Roberto learned to speak German, French, English, Spanish and Italian fluently.

Burle Marx recalled that when he was six his mother took him to a performance of *Tristan and Isolde* and he enjoyed it so much that he hummed the arias the whole of the next day. It was then that Cecília began to train his voice and develop his talent for singing. He eventually became an excellent baritone and not a party passed without him singing his beloved *lieder*.

His early years were filled with music and play in the sloping garden of his home, with its rocks, waterfalls and orchard. At the age of eighteen, however, he began to have problems with his eyesight and turned his attention to gardening. His family decided to go to Europe to consult eye specialists. They settled in Berlin, at that time one of the most vibrant and modern cities in Europe, with an almost mythical aura for Latin Americans. There, during the Weimar years, Burle Marx

Trier, Germany, birthplace of Wilhelm Marx.

discovered an atmosphere of artistic experimentation and cultural ferment which nurtured and stimulated his creative instincts.

Berlin

The year was 1928. The battle of Modernism was being waged. It was an essentially urban phenomenon, thriving on a period of relative peace and economic progress in Germany that created the technical and material conditions for sustained cultural endeavour. Newly established as a republic – the Weimar Republic, which continued from 1919 until Hitler became chancellor in 1933 – Germany enjoyed improved international relations after World War I, allowing a period of dynamic artistic and intellectual exchange with both East and West. A huge influx of American capital under the Dawes Plan of 1924 underwrote an economic rebirth. Those in charge of finance invested in audacious projects in theatre, opera and architecture and introduced a new policy of urban regeneration.

The arts, fired by an animated critique of society, reflected all these changes and attracted people of all nationalities.

The pioneers of postwar Cubism and Futurism were not rejected or devalued in Germany as they had been in other countries, but incorporated into a mutating society. Elements of Cubism and Fauvism were absorbed into the German Expressionist movement. In 1922, Wassily Kandinsky moved from Russia to join the Bauhaus in Weimar, and the Constructivist artist László Moholy-Nagy arrived shortly afterwards in 1923, the same year that the Dutch De Stijl group exhibited their work in Germany. Founded in 1919 to combine the fine arts with arts and crafts teaching, the Bauhaus quickly adopted a more radical approach, its members declaring: 'Art and technology, a new unity.' They worked towards an integration of all art forms, assimilating new techniques and seeking to fulfil the practical needs of an industrial society.

The Burle Marx family arrived in Europe aboard the liner the *Wesser* in a period of great change. In 1927 Charles Lindbergh had made the first transatlantic flight; radio and cinema documentaries were being developed; Fritz Lang's *Metropolis* and G.W. Pabst's *The Street of Sorrow* were being

Roberto Burle Marx, his brother Walter and Anna Piascek.

The Burle Marx brothers travelling to Berlin on board the *Wesser* in 1928.

shown at the cinema. Photography became an art form in these years and helped to emphasize light (sometimes transparency and sometimes reflection), leaving its mark on other arts like theatre and drawing. The year 1927 also saw the inauguration of a department of architecture directed by Walter Gropius at the Bauhaus, which had moved to Dessau, just outside Berlin, in 1925. The art historian Sigfried Giedion founded CIAM (the International Congress of Modern Architecture) in Switzerland in 1928, with members including Le Corbusier and the Russian artist El Lissitzky, and it soon became central to the development and promotion of the new functionalist style in architecture.

In 1929 Thomas Mann, author of *Death in Venice*, won the Nobel Prize for Literature for *The Magic Mountain*. Like Burle Marx, Mann was the son of a Brazilian mother and German father and, like the famous landscape designer, music occupied a decisive place in the writer's work. In his books he analysed the spirit of his time and also pondered the role of the artist in society, another preoccupation he shared with Burle Marx.

The changing role of music in modern society brought innovations with it. Greatly influenced by jazz, music began to be used in radio and the cinema and as an instrument of learning. Artists also borrowed from sport and the cult of the body began to spread. A nudist film broke all attendance records in 1925 and Sigfried Giedion published a small book called *Free Life*.

A school of gestural dance flowered within German ballet, combining gymnastics with Isadora Duncan's corporal expression movement. These new forms in turn inspired artists. Kandinsky used the rhythms of the ballerina Greta Palucca and Oskar Schlemmer created the *Triadic Ballet*.

Berlin was ablaze with magnificent theatre, brilliant first performances of operas, political satires and experimental choreography. In the three years following the production of Alban Berg's *Wozzeck* in 1925, more than 150 operas were composed. Burle Marx went to the first night of Stravinsky's *Oedipus Rex* at the Kroll Opera, to a performance of *Es Liegt in der Luft*, a musical comedy with Marlene Dietrich, and to Kurt Weill's *The Threepenny Opera* with words by Bertolt Brecht. Having

The Burle Marx family in Berlin.

at last overcome the problem with his sight, Burle Marx resumed his music studies, believing, at that time, in the expressive power of singing above all else.

He was changed, however, by his encounters with the painters of an artistic movement then spreading through northern Europe: Expressionism. For Expressionist artists, influenced by German Baroque art, colour was charged with meaning, figures were in constant motion, features were distorted and objective reality was subjugated to an exploration of pure vivid tones. But it was the retrospective of a painter who had died in 1890 that really marked Burle Marx's life. Such was the impression it made on him that he abandoned his musical aspirations and took up painting. The artist was Vincent van Gogh. Burle Marx was overwhelmed when he saw how a painter could communicate human passion by liberating colour from form, exploring contrasts of saturated colour and moving away from description. The impact of Van Gogh is not surprising given that Burle Marx was expansive and passionate by nature and came from a country that expresses affection and emotion intensely. He also

Posters in Berlin, 1928.

admired Matisse, the most virtuoso of modern colourists, although more subtle and aware of balance in visual composition than Van Gogh. Burle Marx enrolled in art school, determined to become a painter.

In search of subjects, he began going to the Dahlem Botanical Gardens. There he saw natural environments from different parts of Europe, which he gave the name 'ecological groups'. These were organized on a taxonomic and geographical basis by the botanist Adolf Engler, the director of the gardens. Ironically it was in these hothouses that Burle Marx marvelled at the extraordinary specimens of Brazilian tropical flora, unknown in gardens in Brazil. He was astonished by the beauty and exuberance of these plants, their sculpted forms, the outlandish size of their leaves, the splendour of their colours. In Brazil such plants were spurned in favour of popular foreign species, a fashion imposed by European gardeners working in Brazil. Faced with such a revelation, he decided to work to win recognition for indigenous South American flora.

The political climate started to turn nasty and the fragile democracy of the Weimar

Republic began to crumble. Disaster struck. On 1 May 1929, Berlin was the scene of bloody repression when Nazi storm troopers attacked Communists in Hermannplatz. This was followed by the Wall Street Crash in New York. American investment was repatriated, unemployment shot up and Nazism took hold. The cultural avant-garde came under attack. The Marx family decided to return to Rio.

The underlying political tensions between Left and Right in Weimar Germany had kept artists in a state of constant creative tension that sent traditional bourgeois cultural values reeling. Oskar Schlemmer wrote in 1926 that 'constant anxiety makes people take a stand almost every day on radical issues'.[2] One-and-a-half years of living in Germany was enough for Burle Marx to capture the essence of this committed art, which expressed itself not only in new forms, but also in the idea that creativity could bring artists closer to the community and integrate them into modern society.

Rio de Janeiro

Burle Marx returned to Brazil at a time when Brazilian architects were struggling to throw off the academicism and eclecticism in vogue since the beginning of the twentieth century. They had already moved through various stages: simplifying the neoclassicism introduced in the nineteenth century by the French mission of 1816, of which Grandjean de Montigny was part; applying the Art Nouveau of another Frenchman, Victor Dubugras; and creating a neo-colonial style in an attempt to rescue building traditions already adapted to Brazil. They studied the designs of the European avant-garde, from Futurism to Expressionism, the Bauhaus and above all Le Corbusier, without ignoring the local legacy of eighteenth-century Portuguese Baroque and indigenous architecture. Modern Art Week in São Paulo in 1922, an exhibition of visual arts and literature, was the culmination of their experimentation, consolidating their aims.

Brazilian Modernism's main theoretician was Lúcio Costa, who in 1930 was named director of the National School of Fine Art in Rio. Burle Marx enrolled the same year with the intention of studying architecture. Costa, however, persuaded him to change to the visual arts. Lúcio Costa's passage through

'With each day that passes, I feel more and more that my life is too short to know and explore all the treasures of Brazilian flora.'[3]

Philodendron acuatum near Manaus, Amazonas, watercolour by Margaret Mee, 1977.

the institution was brief but revolutionary. He modified the academically oriented courses, giving them a Brazilian *Modernista* direction. In this he was assisted by the Russian immigrant Gregori Warchavchik - an architect based in São Paulo who was an exponent of the new ideas - and by the German painter Leo Putz, who was a great influence on Burle Marx's painting. A few months were enough to make a generation of future architects sensitive to the new ideas of the European avant-garde. Burle Marx was part of their world, and it was with them that he eventually worked.

Most of the early projects that these architects undertook were initiated by the government while a property boom created further opportunities. World War II brought a period of rapid prosperity to Brazil, supplier of primary products to the nations at war. Fuelled by economic progress, civil construction reached a peak. Building fever, industrialization, rapid urbanization and rampant inflation all occurred simultaneously.

Influenced by European Rationalism, the Brazilian architects created a functional architecture, although the desire to express themselves in formal terms triumphed over a strict adherence to reason. Brazilian architecture is propelled by the emotions, by the subconscious. It is an architecture of the grand gesture. At the same time it uses what technology has to offer. Burle Marx joined this modern architecture movement because he identified with its rejection of academicism, its respect for function and the way it valued local culture.

In his student years Burle Marx moved within intellectual circles, associating with writers like Oswald de Andrade - high priest of the Pau Brasil movement - and Guimarães Rosa; with the painter Zelia Salgado, the filmmaker Humberto Mauro, art critics, set designers - all of them searching for a national identity. By chance, he lived on the same street as Lúcio Costa. Impressed by the Marx family's garden, in 1932 Costa suggested that Burle Marx should design a garden for the house that Costa and Warchavchik were building for the Schwartz family. In this first garden design, sadly no longer in existence today, Burle Marx planted a terrace with beds of American canna, hitherto considered to be common banana trees.

Alberto Cavalcanti, Roberto Burle Marx and Lúcio Costa.

Pampulha Casino by Oscar Niemeyer, 1942-43.

This was the beginning of a long collaboration between Lúcio Costa and Burle Marx, later enriched by Oscar Niemeyer. Their careers took different directions but all three started from the same conceptual base: the desire to create work that would form a model for the transformation of social and economic reality. They all drew inspiration from the landscape and history of Brazil. While Costa achieved a blend of contemporary and traditional ideas, Niemeyer developed a whole aesthetic around reinforced concrete. Somewhere between the two, working first with one, then the other, Burle Marx developed garden designs inspired by colonial and indigenous motifs, playing with form and materials and combining different autochthonous species.

Costa continued his research into Brazilian colonial architecture throughout his professional career in an attempt to provide his country with solutions appropriate to its own reality. While using the open-plan arrangements and *pilotis* advocated by Le Corbusier, he rescued a traditional social space: the balcony. He used the *brise-soleils* (louvred sunshades) typical of Modernist architecture, combining them with traditional blinds (*treliça*[4]), and chose local materials such as wood, tiles (*azulejos*) and bricks. With Oscar Niemeyer he designed the Brazilian Pavilion at the New York World's Fair in 1939, balancing organic and rectilinear forms, using curves to break up right angles.

Attracted by the plastic qualities of reinforced concrete, Niemeyer exploited its possibilities, creating an autonomous and original movement. For the Pampulha Complex, built between 1942 and 1947, with gardens by Burle Marx, he introduced several features that he went on to develop more fully: curved plans, V-shaped roofs, parabolic surfaces, counterbalances of solid and void. Starting from a Rationalist basis, he investigated reinforced concrete's structural properties but he also stressed a poetic dimension with voluptuous forms, treating architecture 'like an expression of the spirit, of poetry'.[5]

Later, in Brasilia, Niemeyer was able to give sculptural emphasis to volumes that were conditioned by their function, expressing the grandiose aspirations of the urban complex. The arches that feature on

American Canna *Costus* from *Flora Fluminense* by José Mariano da Conceição Fra Velloso (1742-1811).

'The plant is, above all things, dynamic. Its changes prove it is alive.'

'My first gardens in Recife were ecological. I tried to feature the flora of a particular zone, for example, the caatingas[6] *with its cacti.'*

the façades of Niemeyer's Brasilia buildings were sometimes structural, sometimes decidedly decorative. Burle Marx created gardens for these buildings that brought him worldwide fame.

Recife

In 1934 Burle Marx was appointed Director of Parks and Gardens in Recife. There he associated with intellectuals such as the sociologist Gilberto Freyre, the painter Cícero Díaz, the poet and engineer Joaquín Cardoso and critics José and Clarival do Prado Valladares, all of whom shared a way of thinking and feeling and an aesthetic creed.

He also came into contact with the folklore, the mixture of races - Black, Indian and White - and the vast exuberant tropical vegetation of his mother's region, the Brazilian Northeast. The majority of the jungle was still virgin and the landscape of these torrid regions was largely unexplored by Europeans. Consequently the native flora was little used in gardens, even though there were some fifty thousand different species. Since many landowners and their gardeners

were European immigrants who missed their native lands and wanted somehow to re-create them in the Americas, nearly all the plants in both public and private gardens were imported from Europe, with European gardens as their models.

The Praça Paris, a square in Rio created in 1930 by Alfred Agache, is an obvious example. It was designed in a French style and Agache introduced a tree from Malaysia, the Indian almond *Terminalia catappa*, no doubt chosen because its leaves dry to orange hues reminiscent of autumn, a season which does not exist in the tropics. A few Brazilian plants, like bougainvilleas, were reintroduced from Europe, where they had been taken by scientific explorers who came to the Americas in the nineteenth century - Sainte Hilaire, Martius and Humboldt, among others.

Burle Marx stated his 'intention to move away from Romantic European models, allowing gardens to evolve on a par with humanity'.[7] His public and private gardens emphasized the ecological by using the local flora, guaranteeing that the plants blended harmoniously with the soil and the climate.

Aquatic garden for the Casa Forte in Recife, 1935.

'Then I made an aquatic garden which I divided into three parts, one with South American plants, another with Amazonian plants and another with foreign plants.'

Return to Rio

In 1937 Burle Marx left his post in Recife and returned to Rio de Janeiro, where he associated with the avant-garde and took up his painting studies again. He worked as an assistant on the murals that his teacher, Cándido Portinari, was painting at the Ministry of Education and Health. This building – the work of a team of young architects, including Lúcio Costa, Oscar Niemeyer, Luis Nunes, Affonso Reidy, Jorge Machado Moreira, Carlos Leão and Ernani Vasconcellos – became a manifesto for the principles of Le Corbusier, who was invited to work on the project as consultant. Together they designed an independent structure which demonstrated the 'Five Points of a New Architecture' defined by Le Corbusier in 1926: the raising of the building on load-bearing columns (*pilotis*) leaving the ground-level open for circulation; the free arrangement of the façade, made possible by the liberation of the walls from any load-bearing function; the use of horizontal strip windows; open-plan arrangement of the interior; and the inclusion of roof gardens. The building also made extensive use of

Ministry of Education and Health, Rio, 1936-45, now the Ministry of Education and Culture (MEC).

another key feature of Le Corbusier's architecture: *brise-soleils* shading the windows. The building became a reference point for world architecture. Throughout 1938 Burle Marx designed both the green spaces on the ground floor, given over to pedestrians, and those on the terraces.

Meanwhile, he continued to paint. In 1941 he won the Gold Medal for Painting at the National School of Fine Art's exhibition. It was the first of many honours that he was to receive in his life, both in Brazil and abroad.

Another important design project was the Araxá Thermal Park of 1943, which reproduced the phytogeographic zones of the state of Minas Gerais. It was designed with the botanist Henrique Lahmeyer de Mello Barreto, who became Burle Marx's mentor. From him Burle Marx learned the practice of studying plants *in situ* before embarking on a design. He accompanied Barreto on expeditions, called '*coletas*', to find rare species, learning to collect and transport them. He discovered the relationships formed between plants, stones and animals – that no living being exists in isolation, each having various ways of communicating with its fellow

'The zoological gardens will show the reality of nature, the existence of such an intimate link between certain plants and certain animals that I would call them twinned animals-plants.'

'The beak of a hummingbird is so fashioned that it seems specially made to collect nectar from the flower of a bromeliad or a parrot flower.'

Drawing for the Araxá Thermal Park, built in 1943.

beings and the other species that share the same ecosystem.

Burle Marx applied all this knowledge to the creation of his gardens. He sensed that places speak for themselves, that each is unique. He knew how to capture the spirit of a place, discovering the dominant lines, the mysterious undercurrents, deferring to them to create the garden like a composer, in harmony with the landscape.

One way of displaying the spirit of a place in all its splendour was, of course, to use plants native to the region. The difficulty arose when he had to provide these plants: as there was no demand, the species he needed for his plant palette were not available on the market.

He eventually decided to grow the plants himself to avoid relying on commercial channels and he looked for a place with optimum conditions for acclimatizing groups of plants from the diverse regions of Brazil. In 1949, he and his brother Siegfried bought an estate, Santo Antônio da Bica - Saint Anthony of the Spring - an old country house with coffee and banana plantations at Guaratiba, in the state of Rio de Janeiro. The 365,000 square metres of land became his laboratory,

Burle Marx on his estate, Santo Antônio da Bica, in 1950.

where he installed his collection of plants and plotted their evolution.

Journeys

The same year, 1949, Burle Marx began his own expeditions into the interior of Brazil from which he would return with unknown plants. More than twenty species were named after him by the botanists that classified and published them.[8] With every *coleta*, his designs took on more ecological coherence. His gardens were achieving what in scientific terms is called phytocenosis - when groupings of plants that live together in a specific place within an ecosystem reach the maximum stage of their evolution and form stable communities.

His collection grew, demanding ever greater organization, more husbanding, better monitoring. Like any good collector, he fell in love with different families of plants. First he adored the *Araceae*. Then he was mad about *Heliconiaceae*. Later on he had a passion for *Orchidaceae, Begoniaceae, Bromeliaceae, Marantaceae*.

In 1947 he toured Japan and Europe and from then on he was unstoppable. There were

The Kronsfoth Garden of 1955, renovated by its owner, Ralph Camargo, in 1987.

On *coleta* with the painter Margaret Mee.

working trips, garden designs, conferences, but also marvellous opportunities for bringing back new plants to add to his collection. Once, when he was planning a trip to the Philippines, he was advised not to go because political unrest made it dangerous for tourists. Nothing would dissuade him, however. He was determined to bring back specimens of rare orchids for his collection.

These trips influenced the composition of his gardens. He began mixing autochthonous plants with foreign plants from compatible ecosystems. With these combinations he began creating strange gardens, reconstructing distant landscapes or transforming them by incorporating elements from different parts of Brazil and the rest of the world. His profound knowledge of the behaviour of each plant in relation to soil, climate and mutual compatibility, meant he could play with differences, creating perfectly balanced groups of plants. He himself invented an ironical phrase to define these gardens: 'artificial ecological associations'. The harmony and unity he achieved with these mixtures was so perfect that people who didn't know the origin of each plant

thought they were seeing the faithful reproduction of a natural environment. I would call them 'unprecedented associations'; for instance when he planted palm trees from Madagascar beside other palms originally from Puerto Rico and Haiti.

Colonization of Brazil brought a destruction of nature that intensified over the years at an alarming rate. Natural environments are in a state of continual change. Endemic species[9] disappear every day, even before they have been identified. Burle Marx's concern for protecting and conserving nature led him to organize his work systematically as a way of fighting this devastation.

He possessed an amazing intuition for discovering new plants. He formed expedition groups of architects, botanists, geographers and horticulturists and the fame of his *coletas* attracted specialists from all over the world. They accompanied him on trips covering thousands of kilometres to hugely rich unexplored areas that were becoming increasingly difficult to find. With the permission of the government or private landowners, they collected plants that needed studying in order to save them.

On *coleta* with Lucía Cedrón, 1989.

On *coleta* with the landscape architect Leland Miyano.

'In nature there are environmental solutions that quite clearly express life as a form-function binomial. For example, the Ceiba erianthos, *with its huge root concentrated in a very small piece of ground, is an impressive sight. It is equilibrium in disequilibrium.'*

'And what about the Merianthera, *with branches in the shape of stiff fingers, which have the function of storing food and water for hard times.'*

'And certain cacti, Cephalocercus fluminensis, *that writhe over rocks like furry snakes and, in the appropriate season, open into a magnificent but ephemeral flower, prelude to bearing fruit to perpetuate life.'*

On *coleta* in Espírito Santo.

Botanized *in situ*, the plants were then sent all over the world to be identified by experts of that particular family. Whenever possible, Burle Marx collected seeds, roots, shoots and sometimes even large specimens, which he hoped to be able to acclimatize. Once everything was labelled and packaged, it was transported by air or road.

When they reached Burle Marx's estate, the plants were quickly prepared for acclimatization and reproduction. The land at Santo Antônio da Bica is on a slope, has many springs, and offers a variety of environments – sunny or shady, dry or humid – suitable for vegetation with different needs. The nursery gardens cover 6,000 square metres. They are open-air sites protected from the sun by plastic netting, which filters the sunlight to varying degrees according to the environment to be reproduced. Burle Marx also installed 'mist producers' to accelerate root growth.

In this way Burle Marx built up a pioneering laboratory which, as well as supplying plants for his gardens, provided the public with previously unknown species, stimulating a new demand. Some of the specimens he gathered remained in his house as part of

the collection that he later donated to the nation, estimated at more than 3,500 species.

Legacy

I leave to various futures (not to all) my garden of forking paths. JORGE LUIS BORGES

In 1954, Burle Marx lectured in landscape architecture for a short period at the Rio de Janeiro Faculty of Architecture, the only time he ever taught within an academic framework. He was, however, a generous man and during his lifetime he trained dozens of landscape architects who, like myself, came to work in his studio. Invited by the world's most prestigious institutions, he also participated in hundreds of conferences.

Although many people make gardens similar to his, I don't think his teaching was only formal. I consider myself a Burle Marx disciple for other reasons, which could be called ethical. Because, as well as a landscape designer, architect, researcher, musician, painter and sculptor, Burle Marx was a philosopher. Long before ecological awareness became the fashion, he developed a new way of thinking about nature. The spirit of his

The team in Serra do Cipó, 1989.

approach was not to dominate nature but to understand and admire it. His work was never a purely aesthetic concern; it was an attempt to reveal nature's beauty and create harmony between the natural environment and human life. He was convinced that only by achieving a symbiotic coexistence between man and nature would the world become a better place.

In 1955 his practice became Burle Marx Cía Ltda and took on other landscape architects: Fernando Tábora, Julio Pessolari and John Stoddart. With these partners he opened an office in Caracas in 1956 to create both public and private gardens in Venezuela. The office closed in 1964, although Burle Marx continued to work on projects in Venezuela.

He formed another association in 1965, this time with two young architects: José Tabacow, who worked in the studio until 1982, and Haruyoshi Ono, henceforth his lifelong colleague and associate in many different professional activities. He also worked with two São Paulo architects, Koiti and Klara Mori in 1977. After a short apprenticeship, they collaborated with him on his landscaping work, setting up exhibitions and conferences over a period of four years.

Collecting was his passion. As well as his plants, which he hoarded obsessively with the typical collector's desire to complete a series, he also bought handicrafts, pre-Columbian pottery from Peru, art books, semi-precious stones from Brazil and shells from seas the world over.

In March 1985, Burle Marx donated all his property to the state of Rio de Janeiro, including his art collection, library and local handicrafts collection. It became the Roberto Burle Marx Foundation. The work of classifying and organizing the donation was initially done by José Tabacow and then by the landscaper Fátima Gomes, directing a team of fifty employees, before Roberio Dias – another of Burle Marx's collaborators – became director. The house, garden and collection have now been named a site of national heritage.

While happy to have ensured the survival of these fragile riches, Burle Marx nonetheless found it hard to stomach the rhythm imposed by a bureaucracy which forced him to change his much more dynamic way of working. He was not a man to retire quietly. Immediately after the Foundation was set up to administer his property, he bought a

Fátima Gomes.

Haruyoshi Ono.

The day Burle Marx bought a new piece of land to begin all over again, 1985.

'Curiosity keeps me alive.'

new piece of land alongside the one he had donated and, at the age of seventy-five, began all over again with the enthusiasm of his youth. He produced and sold the plants for his gardens, renewed his passion for aquatic plants and constructed six new lakes. He was still prepared to go to Hawaii or down the Amazon at the drop of a hat, to search for specimens that interested him.

He died on 4 June 1994. He was eighty-four and had worked until his last breath. He could barely see and walked with difficulty. His last days were devoted more to painting than to gardens, perhaps because he could only appreciate colour close up on his canvas. His other great passion in these final years was water: although always an important element in his gardens, with the passing of the years it attracted him more and more until it became indispensable.

He reminds me of Claude Monet, also a painter and gardener. As Monet grew old, he became more and more interested in water and aquatic plants and in the last twenty years of his life he painted the water lilies in his ponds obsessively, over and over again. Since we are born in water, there may be a relationship between water and old age, as if we are closing a circle; in ancient mythology death is related to underground rivers, boatmen and lakes.

Roberto Burle Marx was a prolific artist. Just reading a list of his works gives us an idea of the enormous volume he produced. There is no better posthumous tribute to him than to take a tour around the city of Rio de Janeiro: it is an open-air museum of works displaying his unmistakable style, one wholly his own. The Praça Senador Salgado Filho at Santos Dumont Airport, the Parque do Flamengo, the gardens of the Museum of Modern Art, the Copacabana Promenade, Rio Business Centre, the CAEMI Foundation Building, the Petrobras Building, the National Economic and Social Development Bank Building, the Largo da Carioca, the Bank of Brazil...

The Smell of Brazil

Latin America is like the taste of guava; it remains in the mouth hours after eating it. GABRIEL GARCÍA MÁRQUEZ

While his work and the estate that he donated to the nation memorialize Burle Marx in concrete form, he also left a more subtle and

With the actress Sonia Braga.

Burle Marx's lifelong friend, César da Silva, and Marta Montero.

Dressing up.

abstract legacy: that of his character and his unique way of thinking.

Roberto Burle Marx was an extrovert with a sunny personality. He always shone at the centre of any gathering. He loved entertaining friends and lavishing hospitality on them. A visit to his garden and house guaranteed joy. Whenever I went to one of his parties I felt as if I had been invited to Versailles by the King.

From the orchid-filled verandah I see, far away on the horizon, the sea. It is dusk; the sun will soon disappear behind that line. Roberto offers us a drink. It is not easy to choose between the many marvellously coloured concoctions of fruit and alcohol. From the nearby chapel comes religious music. When the frogs and cicadas start to sing, a friend from the Northeast sits in the middle of the lawn, lays out her huge white lace skirt, which contrasts with her dark skin, and begins to prepare acarajés *on her portable stove. After tasting one of these delicious morsels, one can't resist rejoining the line for seconds. Roberto dresses up, masquerades, tells stories, recites. In the sitting room, a friend plays the piano and the host's beautiful baritone voice sings Schubert or Mahler. Behind the house, his* atelier *is decorated with plants winding around the chandeliers, from which orchids hang. Flanked by vertical floral arrangements, like the candelabras in a Baroque church, is a long table, used by day for painting on cloth, and one of these cloths now covers the table. On it is a profusion of tempting dishes, prepared over many days, made with lobsters, prawns, fish and fruit brought specially from all over Brazil.*

Responsible for these parties was César da Silva, Burle Marx's cook since 1974, his great friend, his constant companion, the person closest to him, who looked after him to the end. He knew how to organize a banquet and every one of Burle Marx's birthdays (to which hundreds of guests were invited) was a real fiesta. Also, like a juggler, he could improvise a kitchen during a *coleta*, as I saw in the middle of the *sertão,* an arid region in Bahía. Wherever he was, he could create an elaborate meal, rich in spices, with unforgettable smells.

Burle Marx also cooked with real flair. He was once invited, along with other chefs, to invent recipes for a big hotel in Rio. In his own house he supervised every detail, handing out the odd instruction: 'If sight accompanies taste, the taste is heightened, even more so if the expectation of what one is going to savour anticipates the desire.' I once heard César and Roberto discussing a salad made with lobster. The sauce that accompanied the dish made everything pink, so that it was impossible to distinguish the different ingredients. 'We need to see what we eat. If we know that we're eating lobster, the salad will be doubly tasty,' concluded the host.

Night has fallen and the springs and waterfalls are murmuring. The musicians arrive and cover the burble of water with their folk songs. It is time to dance and sing until we drop.

In his youth, intellectuals and artists attended Burle Marx's parties. Later politicians and millionaires came too. He was surrounded by hordes of people, not only because his personality acted like a magnet but also because of his prestige and power. Numerous little quarrels broke out around him, as if at court or in a guild,

everyone fighting for the privilege of being closest to him. He enjoyed his friendships very much. One of the things he found most painful about reaching such an advanced age was losing so many friends. Each new death was a tremendous blow for him.

He also enjoyed the company of ordinary people, having fun with gardeners, drivers and workmen, who brightened his life with a sense of brotherhood. He admired the boundless creativity that stems from poverty and deprivation and sustains people through hardship. But he detested the resignation that sometimes manifests itself in religious attitudes. He used to say: 'The human condition depends on oneself, not on divine will.'

One of Burle Marx's great talents was his ability to adapt. I saw him readily accept invitations to stay in castles during his travels in Europe, yet just as happily sleep in a hammock in the open air on one of his *coletas* in virgin jungle, or resign himself to spending the night in a grubby hotel with no bath after a day of sun and dust. But having had the chance to live in other countries, he considered it essential to remain in his own.

Flower arrangements in Burle Marx's painting studio.

'I remember a trip I made to Espírito Santo. Penetrating the region of Pancas, I was astonished by the local morphology – a series of conical mountains surrounded the valley, in which the river was a green serpent.'

'We found black stick lilies which challenged us by their need to change, subject to the fluctuations in the weather and humidity; at times retiring, losing colour, turning yellow; and then, after a rainfall, becoming a vivid luminous green and opening into a flower so lovely that Martius, moved by the spectacle, named them "Lily of the Mountain".'

Living abroad was the one case where adapting seemed to him to be harmful. He regretted not having succeeded in persuading his brother Walter, a composer, to return from Philadelphia, where he emigrated in 1940. 'People who live abroad cannot truly express the reality of Brazil, because they don't "smell" the sweat of the Brazilian,' he said.

He always showed a deep desire to create a South American art, an art of world stature that would also unite the continent's cultures and races, a universal message that would still bear his unique imprint.

In Brazil the flora and fauna are exuberant, but also fearsome and mysterious. They terrified the colonizers, who considered them enemies, calling the Amazon 'the green hell'. Vast, immense, the jungle still provokes anguish. Burle Marx transformed the sense of fear and the urge to destroy into love and respect for the vegetation he considered a source of life. He observed, tried to understand, the laws of nature which fascinated him and formed the centre of his world. His eyes knew how to interpret these lessons. He let himself

be carried away by the fascination the environment held for him. His enjoyment of this beauty was almost mystical. Each time he planted something, he felt the excitement and joy of a birth. The imposing, aggressive and sensuous world of nature became tolerable because he humanized it. Burle Marx created gardens on a human scale - ordered, serene, calming.

Post-colonial Latin American society had no collective tradition in the art of gardening. The destruction of trees left many people indifferent. They were convinced everything would grow again, lulled into false security by the extraordinary ability of tropical vegetation to renew itself. They did not know that every living thing is vulnerable. Even as fires rage through the length and breadth of the land, the idea that the jungle is immortal mistakenly persists. For aboriginal peoples, on the other hand, nature has always been a primordial force, wise and provident. Burle Marx improved on this tradition and, by his example, drew attention to mistakes and set out new paths to follow.

Vellozia burle-marxii.

Through his work, he aimed to reveal the identity of the Brazilian people, to value their roots. He believed in the collective destiny of a work of art and the social role of landscape architecture: 'Through the garden we can reconquer time and regain the lost unity of plants and man.' He was convinced that beauty is a kind of catharsis that leads to an understanding of nature and, as a result, curtails vandalism.

'I believe in instinct, albeit controlled, so that once the composition is finished there is nothing to add or take away'; that was his definition of art. Burle Marx saw science as a valid instrument of art, favouring botany, zoology and geology, which he considered to be the sciences closest to man. Although he always questioned his work *a posteriori*, he acted without much prior deliberation. He began constructing in a practical way, finding solutions which he then incorporated into his theories as he went along. He wanted to enhance the culture he inherited and this gave his work a sense of mission.

He was as profuse a writer and lecturer as he was an artist and was often controversial – his denunciations threatened vested interests and irritated people. Today, thanks to the media, his name and work are recognized in every corner of his own country and around the world. Interpretations of his gardens, some serious, some not, have filled the pages of books and magazines. His work is very popular and much copied.

He used to say he had received a lot and that, consequently, it was his duty to give and so help create a different world. He was convinced that, given a different framework, society could and should be better. He worked tirelessly to bring all these ideas to fruition and in this he was aided by his boundless energy and constant optimism.

When creating his gardens, he began by expressing the essence: 'The feel of a composition for a convent is intrinsically different from the feel of the composition for a school.' Inspiration can spring from the memory evoked by a perfume, a taste or a birdsong at night. The artist re-creates a space remembered from the past, or perhaps seen in a dream. In Burle Marx's own words: 'The essence is no more than an elusive emotion.'

Indians meeting European Explorers, engraving from *Voyage pittoresque au Bresil*, by J.M. Rugendas, 1835.

'I would like to warn those who are unaware of what is happening that we are destroying an inheritance that is not ours but belongs to generations to come.'

'If a museum had a fire, everyone would lament the loss. Meanwhile millions of trees are being destroyed – some of them more than five hundred years old – in the face of total indifference.'

The Kronsfoth Garden of 1955, now Pedra Azul.

'Certain principles guide us but we must not confuse them with formulae. Each composition must convey the particular features of each case.'

The Avant-Garde

Ornamentation is crime. ADOLF LOOS

At the same time that he sought to bring as much as possible to those around him, Burle Marx was also receptive to the ideas of others, particularly artists. He adhered to the concepts of visual experience adopted by the early-twentieth-century European avant-garde, finding these a good channel for expression. In Van Gogh's painting he had seen that intensity and contrast of colour can express emotion. The Expressionists revealed to him what was to be his great European discovery: that colour, like form, can evoke rhythm and movement. From Cézanne he learned to imitate deep order and not surface disorder, seeking the geometric structure contained in a landscape. Like Cézanne, he would try to reconstitute colour, since it does not exist by itself, independently of the object or space, but depends on the relative position of the perceiver and the perceived.

The search for form led him to explore ethnographic art, as had Braque and Picasso, and to abstract from the human body and nature, like Arp and Kandinsky. Like Miró,

he developed a language of pictorial signs and abandoned easel painting to experiment with other scales and materials. He appreciated the ludic approach of Klee, with whom he identified in not wanting to be restricted by any kind of formula nor to sacrifice pleasure to concept. He wrote: 'The need for self-expression must precede a work of art.' Keeping faith with this ideal, his aesthetic resembles the lyrical abstraction of the postwar period, represented by Bram Van Velde, Vieira da Silva and the painters of the Ecole de Paris: abstraction indissolubly linked to sensitivity.

He applied to his work a vocabulary that developed the innovations of Cubism: perceptive simultaneity, volumetric interpenetration, transparency, asymmetry and the use of collage. The notion of space-time is evident in his gardens. 'To know a garden you need to walk round it, observe it from different angles,' said Walter Gropius on a visit to a Burle Marx garden. Burle Marx's creations have neither general perspectives that encompass everything nor views that imply only one determinate way of looking at them.

He used primary colours to achieve, through their universal properties, an accessible visual language. He created large monochrome blocks of plants, repeating a species as well as grouping similar kinds of plants to emphasize their common elements. Always he sought economy of expression and hated ornamentation, quoting the architect Mies van der Rohe: 'In architecture, less is more.' When art works were incorporated into his gardens – murals, sculptures, tapestries – they were each conceived for a particular place and created so that they would link to form an organism, following Le Corbusier's concept of designing every element of a complex. Examples of this are the group of sculptures in the lake at the Ministry of the Army in Brasilia (page 124) and the mural for the garden at the Olivo Gomes Residence (page 148).

'Our green is dark, almost black, and by strange contrast it allies itself with two dominant colors: the yellow of Cassia *and trumpet trees* Tabebuia, *which adds vibrancy to the chromatic composition; and the violet of the glory bushes or* quaresmeiras [10] Tibouchina, *almost tailor-made to evoke the ritualistic atmosphere of Holy Week, repeating the liturgical colour of the services and processions. Nature displays these unique colours together, making them compete with the rose tones of the floss-silk trees* Chorisia *to add measure to the composition. These are colours that only express themselves in that particular light, against that sky, in contrast to the dark and dense green of the jungle around them. We also find, in the shape and rhythm of the mountains and hills, an allegro vivace which contrasts with moments of contemplation, the adagio of the valleys and planes.'*

Chapter Two
The Artist

Drawing in India ink from the *Erotica* series, 1983.

[Burle Marx's] brushstroke, be it light, strong, tender, dense or fiery, is always full of latent visual significance.
LÚCIO COSTA

If any one work by Burle Marx is to be understood, it cannot be isolated from the rest of his *oeuvre*, nor can any single aspect be analyzed and others ignored. The tendency to classify that developed during the twentieth century means we differentiate between, and sometimes contrast, the different manifestations of art. We disregard superimpositions, diversity, identification and create arbitrary barriers. In Burle Marx's case, there was a constant dialogue between his landscape design and his visual art, with one art form continually feeding the other. The importance of his prolific and diverse work lies precisely in the fact that he was landscape designer, painter and musician at one and the same time. And painting, sculpture and architecture all came together in his gardens.

As well as painting in oil and acrylic, he created line drawings in India ink. To reach a wider audience he made engravings, serigraphs, lithographs and print reproductions on paper of his paintings. His boundless inventiveness extended far beyond his canvases: he designed theatre sets, ceramic murals, concrete reliefs, sculptures and tapestries. He also turned his attention to everyday household objects far removed from the conventional art market, designing tablecloths, fabric prints, jewellery, cushions, glass ornaments, patterns for stained glass and so on.

Another of his techniques was to arrange mini-gardens, reminiscent of Japanese *ikebana*, composed of flowers, fruits, leaves, stones, feathers, branches, thorns, vegetables, seeds, wood and painted bamboo. Using powerful imagery, the arrangements evoked as much emotion as a landscape or a garden. These small works of art brought out both the sculptor and the gardener in Burle Marx.

Fruit arrangement.

Burle Marx's formal repertory was nourished by the mixture of cultures and the abundant nature native to Brazil. These inexhaustible sources of form, colour and sound inspired him to break with the aesthetic of imitating reality. Moving away from European academicism, he turned to ethnographic art and popular imagery. He freely incorporated local elements into his designs, drawing on pre-Columbian graphics and architecture, rhythms from Black art and features of Iberian gardens in Brazil. From Portuguese gardens – in turn inflected by foreign influences, especially under Arab domination – he took an emphasis on water, mosaic floors of black and white stone called Portuguese stone (adapted from a Roman technique) and ceramic tile walls (originating from Persian art). With marble and granite scavenged from demolition sites, he built walls, façades and planters. He collected traditional crafts, putting them on a par artistically with 'highbrow art', but at the same time appreciating their practical features.

Prompted by the exuberant formal and chromatic power of his work, some writers describe Burle Marx's gardens as paintings. The English landscaper Gertrude Jekyll evoked a similar reaction from critics, who called her gardens 'living pictures'. There are also those who see gardens in Burle Marx's paintings. Both his art and his gardens reflect the vivid contrasting colours of his country's flowers, leaves, bird plumage and butterflies, as well as the sinewy, voluptuous shapes of Brazilian bodies, the bare hills polished by time, and the coast sculpted by the sea.

His painting did not suddenly throw off figurative conventions; it gradually moved towards abstraction over time. Burle Marx initially found inspiration in the natural world because it offered an infinity of pure, non-narrative forms. Later, he sought to capture the spirit of the material universe, abstracting pictorial forms from real ones. For example, some of his abstract India ink drawings have complex lines that hint at ambiguous anatomical contours, as in the series he called *Erotica*.

Painting on cloth, 1985.

Moulded concrete relief panel for the São Paulo Confederation of Industry, 1969.

A group of *Pithecolobium tortum*, Parque do Flamengo.

Pithecolobium tortum, India ink drawing, 1964.

Critics alternatively label his work figurative or abstract, according to whether they can perceive its origin in the real world. This ambiguity led the art critic Clarival Valladares to describe Burle Marx's painting as 'figurative abstraction'.[11] Comparing photographs of trees with drawings by Burle Marx in his book *The Tropical Gardens of Burle Marx* (1964), Pietro María Bardi pointed out the underlying references to the plant world in those apparently non-figurative drawings. Flávio Motta, in his 1984 book *Roberto Burle Marx e a nova visão da paisagem* (*Roberto Burle Marx and the New Vision of Landscape*), discovered branches and bark hidden in Burle Marx's canvases. Similarly, the French art critic Jacques Leenhardt wrote in *Burle Marx, uma poética da modernidade* (*Burle Marx, Poetry of Modernity*) of 1989: 'His paintings are gardens where the spirit wanders, just as his gardens are drawings where nature takes shape.'

Launched into this adventure with form, Burle Marx realized that everything around him could be a source of inspiration for his work, from the veins of a leaf to an advertising billboard or an architectural detail.

Paintings and Gardens

Whether Burle Marx expressed his emotions with elements of nature or with a paintbrush, the common denominator was always his desire to create a work of art. When conceiving his gardens he used visual elements, among others, employing the same principles that dominated his painting. This has led to some rather confused interpretations of his work and meant that other important components, such as his use of space, have been ignored. However, the evolution of his visual art and his gardens clearly coincide.

In his early paintings, the subject was the focal point, just as it had been in his first gardens. Clarival Valladares described this approach as 'the sanctification of the object'.[12] A rejection of academicism had led Burle Marx to choose popular scenes and figures from Brazil as his themes - Blacks, Creoles, servants, the shanty towns

Portrait of Black Woman, oil on paper, 1935.

Mangroves: drawing for Praça do Derby, 1935.

and surrounding granite hills. At a time when only European themes were considered important, this promotion of local culture was a radical stance. In his gardens, his fascination with Brazil's plants led him to use cacti, water lilies *Victoria amazonica* and screw pines *Pandanus utilis* as framed monuments or grouping them in ecological associations to make a feature of them as if they were the real protagonists of the design.

During the 1940s, his attention shifted from the narrative to the purely visual. In his art works, subject became subordinate to composition, areas of colour became divorced from descriptive outline. These changes in his painting influenced his garden designs: plants were arranged in large monochrome blocks, following undulating biomorphic shapes. At the same time, he improved his knowledge of botany and this contact with the plant world influenced in turn his visual vocabulary. These developments reached a peak in the garden for Olivo Gomes (page 148), on which he began work in 1950. Burle Marx incorporated two murals made of

tiles, inspired by the massing of coloured plants in the herbaceous borders. These were his first abstract works, created long before he painted anything abstract on his easel.

The Italian architecture critic Bruno Zevi, who considered Burle Marx the greatest contemporary landscape designer, wrote in 1957: 'His gardens are paintings made with plants which serve to correct architecture, to humanize it...Reconciliation of the pure geometry of Rationalist architecture and the curves of luxuriant tropical nature is achieved through the experience of modern painting.'[13] Zevi sites Miró and Arp as examples. He observed that on the terraces of the Ministry of Education and Health in Rio the free forms of the planters play the role of 'psychological compensators'[14] by destroying the rectangle. These observations were written before the Italian critic had seen other designs by Burle Marx which follow the perpendicular structures of Rationalist architecture, such as the gardens of Rio's Museum of Modern Art (page 72), and the gardens of the University City in São Paulo (page 40).

Plan of the Ministry of Education and Health roof garden, 1938.

Cais (Quay), oil on canvas, 1941.

Plan of the University City in São Paulo, 1953.

Later on, Brazil's own modern architecture steered away from the 'angle droit'.[15] The rejection of the 'right angle' threw Brazilian architects into a world of daring shapes. Burle Marx's wavy lines not only reflected nature, they also expressed the spirit of a whole people. His was an art of instinct; his murals never attempt to soften the weight of an empty wall by playing the role of trompe-l'oeil. The way he transformed architecture corresponded to his own need to express himself, which he did at every possible opportunity.

Clarival Valladares maintains that Burle Marx used plants as if they were pigments and the ground like a canvas. Burle Marx agreed with this interpretation at one stage but subsequently saw in landscape architecture a highly developed and autonomous art form with a living, mutating raw material and characteristics all its own: light, movement and development over time. One fact in particular contradicts those who claim Burle Marx made 'living pictures': the position of each garden and the natural environment surrounding it is unique. Burle Marx paid particular attention to geographical and topographical features. His gardens could only be created on the land specified for each design. As Frank Lloyd Wright noted, each place has its own formal language.

Moreover, Burle Marx's unfold over time, like music. If each coloured form corresponds to a sound, the composition as a whole expresses harmonies and dissonances. The musical essence of this world of forms led him in turn towards expressive lyrical paintings which became increasingly abstract.

In the 1950s, Burle Marx was asked to direct several large urban projects and he worked in collaboration with architects. His priorities shifted from painting to garden design. However, his contact with architecture prompted the introduction of pure geometry, both in his gardens and in his painting, giving prime importance to an emphasis on planes. He did not consider natural forms and geometrical forms to be in opposition. Observing a flower, a spider's web or a

Copacabana Promenade, 1970.

Acrylic on canvas, 1968.

Flower arrangement.

Acrylic on canvas, 1985.

crystal, he said, reveals a physical universe that obeys mathematical laws.

To critics who suggested that the plants in his beds had no intrinsic quality and existed only to define a contrast, Burle Marx replied that 'the uniformity of large surfaces made up of a single plant type is broken by the detail in each individual plant'. The rigidity of the flower beds was destroyed by the exuberance of the tropical plants and by paths crossing between them, providing views from various angles. In *Burle Marx, uma poética da modernidade*, Lélia Coelho Frota writes: 'His gardens become geometrical...At the same time, the way the plants grow, their dynamic tridimensionality, their colour, their texture, the effect of light and wind on them, gradually turn the initial design into a single entity, in which the work of the artist and nature itself start to merge, entering into a dialogue, dissolving.'

During the 1960s, Burle Marx was commissioned to design more and more urban schemes. He worked on important projects in cities all over Latin America – Caracas, Brasilia, Santo André, Buenos Aires –

continuing his tireless search for form in experiments with interpenetrating curves and straight lines. It was at this stage that his paintings became totally non-figurative, a decade after the abstract murals in the Olivo Gomes garden, which clearly exerted a reciprocal influence on his painting. He began to incorporate pattern and to use collage, in which he was able, with only a slight shift in the composition, to create a field of tension. Painting once again came to occupy pride of place in his creative production. His drawing became increasingly suggestive, full of complex, irregular Baroque lines. His painting took on the suggestion of depth, incorporating the representation of space in which volumes floated. His gardens also became more volumetric and he created objects with materials other than plants.

At the beginning of the 1980s, Burle Marx began to devote more time to his easel than to the drawing board (although the dialogue between them never died) perhaps as an impotent reaction to a world in crisis. Colour – increasingly vibrant and violent, always

'How strange it is to see how certain primitive forms of art are based on an observation of nature.'

'There are illuminating analogies. A spoon is the spathe – the bag that wraps the flower of an arum lily; a hook can be the thorn of a palm tree – a Desmonchus *perhaps, the climbing palm that latches on to trunks, branches, lianas to help it climb.'*

'Similarly, much more elaborate works, like Pier Luigi Nervi's structures, can be seen in the intricate vein system of the leaves of a Victoria regia*.'*

'I want to stress that nature is a symphony where the elements are intimately related; size, form, colour, movement, perfume and so on.'

sensual and erotic – began to dominate, as if this could ameliorate his suffering over the gradual loss of his sight. Painting gave him great pleasure.

Circular Paths

Burle Marx studied nature; he wanted to learn the secret of its beauty. His work followed a circular path. He would record what he saw, observing light and shade, sometimes capturing the shadow of a pergola, making a minute study of branches and roots, to create patterns, forms and colours. Starting from this observation of reality, his paintings would become essentially abstract. Burle Marx then applied his experience as a visual artist to his landscape designs. When colouring the plans for his gardens, he followed a convention by which certain tones corresponded to the leaves or flowers they represented. These technical drawings came to resemble his paintings. The circle closed when his designs became nature again in his gardens. A chain of interaction was thus established between his landscape work and his paintings: his

The 'Garden of Volumes' at Vargem Grande Fazenda, designed in 1979, shown during construction in 1988.

canvases enabled him to create his gardens as visual art, and his gardens opened the way for a new expressiveness in his painting, enriching and transforming it.

Burle Marx did not intend that his gardens should copy a natural landscape, nor did he want them to be metaphors. He created abstract spaces capturing and expressing the lyricism of a landscape. While his painting interpreted nature and the emotion which nature inspired in him, his gardens relayed that interpretation three-dimensionally over time.

Chapter Three

Landscapes

'I recently found, in the Sincorá mountains in Bahía, a perfect natural garden. There, on lovely ground, lakes and slopes of stratified rock, grew copeys Clusia fluminensis, *with shiny leaves, dark green, a colour echoed in the flamingo plants* Anthurium *and the leaves of certain orchids. There were gold, green and greyish bromeliads, air plants* Tilandsia *– some silvery, others with purplish stripes – tiny spurges* Euphorbia, *small glory bushes* Tibouchina *and some cacti.'*

The creation of a garden is a human activity carried out with elements of nature; human creative will is imposed on nature's development and transforms it through art. Roberto Burle Marx drew a clear distinction between 'existing natural landscape and constructed human landscape'.

The Spirit of the Place

The classical garden is ordered in the extreme, geometric, its forms opposing those of nature. Its purpose is to leave no doubt as to the identity of the creator. André Le Nôtre, designer of the gardens at Versailles, composed his gardens like the painter he had been, seeking to demonstrate both Louis XIV's and his own artistic flair in an intellectual and erudite style, full of allegory, even employing the golden section and mythology. By contrast, the English garden aims to reproduce nature so that all artifice is hidden. The result is described by J. Benoist-Méchin in his book of 1975, *L'homme et ses jardins* (*Man and his Gardens*) as an 'anti-garden'.

Roberto Burle Marx's gardens are strictly ordered, but appear natural and harmonious.

His intimate relationship with nature, the respect it inspired in him, gave rise to spaces that are spontaneous, wild, but at the same time man-made. He conceived his gardens with an internal order of their own, distinct from nature, seen by many to be devouring and powerful. This new and original approach was achieved through an interdependence of materials, shapes and colours. Burle Marx created his gardens with the idea that his own involvement should go unnoticed. For example, he would divert the course of a river so that it looked as if it had always flowed that way. Nevertheless, his style and imprint were always unmistakable, 'Burlesque-Marxist' as he joked.

His early gardens are generally associated with English landscaped gardens because of their formal similarity. Both create tension by bringing varied elements together to provoke surprise and discovery. However, Burle Marx did not seek the simplicity of a blossoming orchard like Jean Jacques Rousseau. On the contrary, his gardens are sophisticated. Although his plant beds were inspired by English mixed borders, where flowers bloom briefly in succession,

An 'existing natural landscape': Pai Inácio Hill at Chapada Diamantina.

'It was a chromatic happening in which the volumes came together and established relationships, the textures of the stones blended with those of the plants. There were linking planes between the stone slabs and the landscape in the valley and you could hear the sound of falling water. The water apart, there was an enormous silence, inhabited by tiny imperceptible sounds making the music of nature, and all around the light was strong but not hard. Nothing was out of place. This is the harmony found in nature.'

he worked with the colours and textures of foliage to achieve a more intense, contrasting and durable effect.

A great admirer of the English garden, he followed the advice of the poet Alexander Pope, who wrote in 1731: 'Always consult the *genius loci*, the spirit of the place, in everything.'[16] There is no doubt that Burle Marx was able to discover this spirit. He would interpret the essence of a place, knew how to extract its character and make it more expressive, highlighting the intrinsic beauty of the scenery so that it served as an exterior backdrop. Every landscape has a special meaning in the eye of the beholder. Burle Marx captured these underlying signs and organized them into a theme to conjure up a state of mind. He was able to create a sense of unity between the garden and its surroundings.

Like voluptuous Arab gardens, in which the different elements are arranged to excite the senses, Burle Marx's gardens are penetrated through sight, sound and smell and also through memory, evoking an emotional resonance in the visitor. His gardens also share with Arab gardens an emphasis on water, which plays a fundamental role, serving to mitigate the heat. As Elizabeth B. Kassler has written about contrasts, when in the desert one longs for the jungle, in the jungle one prefers an oasis of calm, and while the Arab garden pursues a mystical end, the Burle Marx garden seeks an ethical meaning. To discourage the destruction of nature, he sought to create an order where beauty fulfils other functions beyond mere pleasure. In this sense his work is close to Le Nôtre's classical ordered garden. In both, the emphasis is on structure, although Burle Marx has no central axis or symmetry, no sculpted trees or mazes. The real difference between them lies in the role given to the site since, as Benoist-Méchin points out, Le Nôtre 'prefers to turn the site into a garden, not adapt the garden to the lines suggested by the site'.[17]

Burle Marx's compositions also have affinities with Chinese and Japanese gardens, using resources economically, making the most of the texture of minerals, the sculpted shapes of stones, the blooms and, above all, the particular shapes of trunks and branches, so that an energy runs through the garden.

The logogram of Burle Marx's practice.

'A garden, on the other hand, is organized nature, where the artist aims to bring out the beauty of the colours, the forms, the rhythm, the ordered volumes. It is the establishing of harmony, the creating of contrasts, since the whole is a warp and weft in which every element is indispensable.'

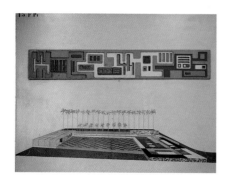

Models for the Francisco Pignatari mural and garden, 1956.

However, in Burle Marx's gardens there are no worlds in miniature or allegories of nature, they are not intended as places to escape and to dream, there is no silence of stillness. His gardens are refined, but the profusion and the abundant tropical vegetation give this refinement an almost violent effect. While formally they resemble Chinese gardens with their interminable spiral paths, they are more like Japanese gardens in their attempt to calm chaos and control anarchy.

Burle Marx's emphasis on the visual has given rise in certain quarters to a Cubist interpretation of his landscapes. In France, at the beginning of the twentieth century, a new way of creating gardens emerged, based on light and colour. Reacting against the naturalism of Art Nouveau, the search for a new approach lay in imposing geometry on nature. André Vera introduced the concept of the *Jardin nouveau* in 1912 and the *Jardin au soleil* in 1919: in these, nature was controlled by using pure lines and forms but without replicating the gardens of the past. Art became the instrument to create the antithesis of nature in the garden.

This all came at a time when Cubist artists were experimenting with the deconstruction of the object into its different facets, disregarding the traditional distinction of object from ground and dissolving perspective. The first Orphic[18] Cubist garden, the *Jardin d'eau et de lumière*, was created in 1925 for the Exposition des Arts Décoratifs in Paris. Its designer, the Armenian architect Gabriel Guévrékian, tried to elevate landscaping to the rank of modern painting. He sought to re-create the fundamental experience expressed in Cubist painting of spatial transparency and its decomposition in strata. Paradoxically, he did not manage to make the light omni-directional nor to dissolve perspective in the real space and time of a garden, where the spectator moves horizontally down the terrain.

In 1926 Guévrékian designed a garden in the southeast of France for the Villa Noailles in Hyères (now reconstructed). It was a composition with superimposed planes of different materials, to be observed from another, higher level. The garden was subordinate to the architecture – merely the conclusion of a tour around the house –

and planned in such a way as to provide the best views of the mansion from the green space outside.

The garden that Burle Marx created in São Paulo for Francisco Pignatari in 1956 (now called Parque Roberto Burle Marx) was, for Bruno Zevi, an extension of the architecture. For other critics, the highly geometrical garden, in which the visual element is the most important feature, evokes the Cubist garden, with light playing on the intense colours and moving water to create vibrating rhythms and contrasts.

But Burle Marx's garden differs fundamentally from the classic Cubist garden. To see this we need only look at the way Guévrékian champions architecture over the garden. For Guévrékian, the garden was an object that existed exclusively to be observed. His plant selection was made purely on the basis of colour and shape. Burle Marx's garden does not play second fiddle to the house: the two exist side by side in equilibrium. In all his creations, the plant palette is not independent of the context but has to blend with the natural and cultural environment.

The 'Burlesque-Marxist' Style

No; it was not the amount, but the character of the art which caused me to take a seat on one of the blossomed stones and gaze up and down this fairy-like avenue for half an hour or more with bewildered admiration.
EDGAR ALLAN POE

Burle Marx absorbed the lessons of nature and the many different traditions of landscape design to create his own unique style.

The issue of whether to make clear distinctions or gradual transitions was key to this development. The boundaries of a garden were a source of constant interest for Roberto Burle Marx. How to reconcile architecture, nature and garden? Lúcio Costa saw the garden as an area in which the contradictions between the discipline, rigidity and symmetry of architecture, on the one hand, and the imprecision, movement and asymmetry of nature, on the other, might be resolved. So, do Burle Marx's gardens seek, as Bruno Zevi puts it, to correct architecture? Burle Marx said no: 'The garden is a transition between architecture and landscape.' His gardens used elements from both architecture and

'If the garden is to complement the landscape, it has the landscape as a starting point.'

A 1985 photograph of the Mangrove Fazenda in Rio de Janeiro, created in 1974.

Plan for Praça Terreiro de Jesús, Salvador, 1952.

landscape, which were thereby brought into an alliance that transformed them. It was a process of synthesis.

In his constant search for balance, for harmony, Burle Marx offered specific solutions to this problem for each particular case, sometimes subtle transitions, at other times clear contrasts. In an effort to integrate a garden with its surroundings, he tended to do away with boundaries, following the approach of the invisible 'ha-ha' in the English garden.[19] The outsize dimensions of some of his gardens, kept by armies of gardeners, reflect the enormous extent of his almost continent-sized country.

Despite the wild aspect of Burle Marx's compositions, there was nothing more consciously formalist than their gestation, aiming at a definitive, finished object: a taming of nature which at the same time accepted the unfathomable side of living things but rejected anything alien to his design. He formulated his compositions with the utmost care and rigour, either through drawings on paper in his workshop or on site as the forms actually materialized. Nothing was left to chance.

A quick glance at his plans would suggest that the designs emerged from an impulse, a gesture. However, a deeper reading shows the geometrical rigour with which they were drawn: the centre is shifted to avoid symmetries, there are changes of axis, of direction, causing perpetual breaches.

This rigorous approach was maintained as his work developed over the years, passing through formal variations that exhibited a diverse morphology. Starting in the 1940s with organic, biomorphic forms that paralleled Brazilian gestural architecture. In the 1950s he began to introduce pure geometry in an attempt to work with Rationalist architecture, but he avoided symmetrical axes for which he had a visceral distaste – 'Asymmetry frees the spirit,' he said – and discovered that, although geometry may not represent an actual visual object, it can transmit the real world of emotion. In the 1960s curves and orthogonals interpenetrate and this process of syncretization increased through the 1970s, still preserving an expressive and vigorous poetry, culminating in the eclectic juxtapositions of his final work in

Plan for a fourth-floor terrace at the Pompidou Centre, 1988.

Plan for Parque Ibirapuera, São Paulo, 1953.

'You have to delve deep into the soul of the people, into the Brazilian landscape, and with that vocabulary re-create a new syntax, a new language.'

the 1980s. His last landscape compositions are eclectic. He placed one formal system beside another without transition, juxtaposing contradictory features (in the unbuilt project for Sant'Ana Fazenda of 1987 and in the Biscayne Boulevard project of 1992, for example) to produce an effect of dislocation which brought a dramatic quality to the space.

Burle Marx's style has become fashionable and other landscape architects now attempt to reproduce his sinuous gardens. His aesthetic vision was, however, bound up with his ethical concepts, and purely formal imitations do not always convey the message he wanted to transmit: his plea for man's liberation and solidarity through art. Nevertheless there does exist what could be called an American school, represented by his pupils, disciples and others who adhere to his principles and search for new ways to apply them.

Walls, Floors and Levels

The structure of his compositions was, in most cases, based on the use of predominant planes. These could be horizontal, vertical or oblique according to the terrain and became the central feature of the design.

In urban gardens the focal point was usually a large area of paving stones or a wall made into a vertical garden. In some cases, the horizontal plane was emphasized by several parallel planes arranged on different levels, using graduated planters or groups of bushes of different heights. For the Praça Dalva Simão in Belo Horizonte (1973), he devised a pergola supported on cement and steel columns with the beams of its roof jutting out at different angles, covered with vines and creepers of various colours.

Outside the city, the sloping sides of the valleys were either preserved, providing oblique planes which highlighted the characteristic silhouette of the flower beds – which, because of the intricacy of his design, would themselves stand out as a plane in the composition – or dug out in cement terraces which placed the constructed surface against the natural profile. In some cases the plants themselves create virtual planes – colonnades of palm trees in front of a building or opaque curtains of bamboo planted at the boundaries of a garden.

Praça Dalva Simão of 1973 in Belo Horizonte, shown in 1986.

Sketch for the Sant'Ana Fazenda, 1987.

Forms and Volumes

In the tropics trees are gigantic, their trunks covered with epiphytes.[20] Enormous, strangely shaped leaves are often patterned with spots or veins of two or three colours. And in the midst of this dense vegetation, intertwined with the aerial roots of lianas, burst forth spectacular blooms. Many of the plants look robust, with huge, fleshy leaves. Burle Marx's gardens are also densely populated. Over the years, he filled spaces with strange forms, sometimes with plants covering other plants. Alternatively, he grew plants up purpose-built structures. He conceived the volumes in his gardens like a sculptor. The flora grew in beds carved in concave or convex shapes or dangled over the protruding and receding volumes of cement or stone walls. He would use plants to modify silhouettes by training them around the trunks of palms or other trees.

A frequent theme in the city was the garden built on concrete slabs, *jardin sur dalle*, where there was not enough soil for big trees to grow. Burle Marx filled these spaces in a remarkable way, constructing metal or cement forms covered with bark to support plants and incorporating an automatic watering system. These constructions formed virtual plant towers, rising to twelve metres tall. The finished effect was achieved very quickly because plants grow fast in the tropics, reaching maturity within a couple of years, and because the structures were prepared ready for a garden's inauguration.

The landscapes he created are fluid and dynamic. There is a sensation of depth, with the boundaries of the gardens often highlighted like a theatre backdrop. Paths are often arranged to suggest movement and there is a balance between vegetation, mineral and water.

Mineral Textures

In some urban gardens Burle Marx used mineral elements as the main feature of the composition. These provide texture, form and colour and appear in a variety of guises: as *bas-relief* murals in reinforced concrete; as stone walls which support plants or form a base for cascading water; as mosaics using different-coloured Portuguese stone interspersed with marble and granite;

Sketch for the 'Garden of Volumes' at Vargem Grande Fazenda, 1979.

'The amazing thing is that the Baroque and Rococo adapted so admirably to the Brazilian landscape. Brazil is so Baroque you get the impression the style was born here.'

as large rocks standing in isolation like sculptures or in moulded concrete forms inspired by the mineral world; and as street furniture (benches and so on) in reinforced concrete.

Water Sources

Melodic brooks run through them and their ripples reflect the warbling in the throats of the branches.
'The Gardens of Oualata' in *The Garden of Caresses* (anonymous Arab poem)

In Brazil the sensation of heat is constant. The droughts and torrential rains that bring landslides and floods turn water into an obsession. Water is an essential element in all Burle Marx's gardens. He knew how to use its natural forms – rivers, springs and brooks – and when there was none, he created artificial lakes, pools or waterfalls. The transition he created between water and land was gradual: the plants at the water's edge were arranged in undulating bands, evoking the marks left by waves in the sand.

In the lakes of his early gardens, Burle Marx included plants that reproduced quickly in an aquatic environment. As a result, forms and colours soon merged in unpredictable ways and the original composition was lost. To avoid this, he began to construct sub-aquatic planters to limit the plants' growth, restricting the space available and, in time, disciplining the composition.

When it is still, water acts as a mirror or draws an unexpected iridescence from the land. When in motion, it is a vehicle - a way for nature to reach the garden.

Secret Rhythms

Through clever use of proportion and a measured choice of dominant elements, Burle Marx applied the academic language of visual composition to each of his works. He used light and shade in particular to define volume, structure and texture. Sometimes the impression of luminosity was obtained through colour. Burle Marx's compositions were mainly based on the use of primary colours – red, yellow, blue – or violent contrasts – violet flowers beside orange flowers, for example. This is how he expressed sensuality.

'Rhythm is not repetition; it is the relationship between one form and another, one space and another, one texture, one surface, one colour, and another.'

In his gardens the following principles were applied:

Analogy: Different species with common visual features are planted together to show their formal similarity.

Contrast: Surfaces of contrasting colour or texture are juxtaposed to exploit the complementary nature of opposites. Contrast allows the composition to be seen from a distance and is particularly suitable for two new categories of spectator: motorists and the inhabitants of tower blocks.

Repetition: 'The more a saying is repeated, the truer it becomes,' according to an old Oriental adage. Burle Marx grouped plants of similar texture, form and colour for emphasis. For example, he would create large monochrome patches with beds full of the same plant, or plant trees of the same species - chosen for their foliage, blooms or shape - in groups as if they were bouquets.

Isolation: Conversely, certain plants with distinctive features benefited from being planted on their own. This reinforced their individuality, showing them off to their full effect compared to the homogeneous masses around them.

Figure and ground: On a graphic design, pattern and background would be inverted to provoke a dynamic reading, setting up an opposition between a form and its negative.

Expansion-reduction: Burle Marx did not always create his landscaped environments by planting. In certain cases, he achieved the desired effect by taking out certain existing elements or, on other occasions, by augmenting them.

Rhythm: Burle Marx achieved rhythm by recognizing the changeable nature of plants, the cycles of day and night, variations in the light, the noise of water, the wind in the leaves, the fragrances of each season, the controlled balance between a wood and a clearing. Flowers come into bloom at different places through the seasons to evoke movement. Paths were carefully organized to offer a way of reading the composition; their form becomes an invitation to a walk along them; they were designed as a storyboard, a succession of frames, multiplying the viewpoints. The visitor discovers diverse environments that will fire the imagination and produce different states of mind.

'We can use repetitions, analogies, contrasts, approximations, distances, relationships between volumes, surfaces and lines, as well as forms, colours and textures.'

The rhythm of breathing will change
as the visitor walks, going up, going down,
stopping, passing from dense vegetation
to more open spaces. The step quickens,
then stops, as the visitor perceives the music
of the spaces. This unique approach evokes
the music and dance of the Black slaves
whose movements are so much a part
of Brazilians today.

*'If we rely on the laws of composition
(the interplay of volumes, the establishing of
rhythms, the contrast and harmony of forms,
the use of colour) and understand, at the same
time, the dynamism of a plant's vegetative
cycle; if we appreciate the changes in the
daytime cycle from dawn to dusk, through all
its graduations, and at night we use light in
the least conventional and aggressive way; and
if we are also conscious of sounds, murmuring
waters, the wind in the treetops, the fragrances
which mark the seasons, and, above all,
the tenacity of certain species, together with
sociological implications, we will be assured,
through our own efforts, a more balanced
and just life for mankind today.'*

Endnotes to Part One

1. An area in the south of the city. Burle Marx was part of an interdisciplinary team, lead by the architect Juan Kurchan, commissioned by the municipality of Buenos Aires in 1970 to undertake urban regeneration.

2. Oskar Schlemmer, quoted in John Willet, *Les années Weimar* (Paris, F. Hazan, 1984).

3. Unless otherwise indicated, the italic texts in the margins are extracts from seminar papers written by Roberto Burle Marx, some of which are published in *Arte e Paisagem* (*Art and Landscape*) (São Paulo, Editorial Nobel, 1987).

4. Sort of lattice windows, of Oriental origin, adopted in Portugal and brought to Brazil as a result of colonization.

5. Oscar Niemeyer, *Rio* (Rio de Janeiro, Avenir Editora, 1980).

6. Characteristic vegetation of the dry region of the Brazilian Northeast.

7. All Burle Marx quotes come from personal conversations and his book of selected conferences *Arte e Paisagem* (*Art and Landscape*) (São Paulo, Editorial Nobel, 1987).

8. Some of the plants listed below were discovered by Roberto Burle Marx, others were named after him as a tribute:
   Aechmea burle-marxii E. Pereira.
   Aechmea correia-araujei Pereira et Moutinho.
   Aechmea flavo-rosea E. Pereira.
   Aechmea grazielae Martinelli et Leme.
   Anthurium burle-marxii G.M. Barroso.
   Barbacenia minima L.B. Smith et Ayensu.
   Begonia burle-marxii Brade.
   Burlemarxia pungens Menezes et Semir.
   Burlemarxia rodriguesii Menezes et Semir.
   Burlemarxia spiralis Menezes et Semir.
   Calathea burle-marxii H. Kennedy 'Ice Blue'.
   Calathea burle-marxii H. Kennedy 'Snow Cone'.
   Calathea fatimae H. Kennedy (ined).
   Calathea singularis H. Kennedy (ined).
   Chaetostoma burle-marxii Mello Barreto.
   Cryptanthus burle-marxii Leme.
   Ctenanthe burle-marxii H. Kennedy var. burle-marxii.
   Ctenanthe burle-marxii H. Kennedy var. obscura.
   Dyckia burle-marxii L.B. Smith.
   Encyclia burle-marxii Pabst.
   Heliconia adeliana L. Emygdio et Em. Santos.
   Heliconia aemygdiana R. Burle Marx.
   Heliconia burle-marxii L. Emygdio.
   Heliconia marie augustae L. Emygdio et Em. Santos.
   Heliconia pabstii L. Emygdio et Em. Santos.
   Hohembergia edmundoi Smith et Read.
   Hohembergia lanata Pereira et Moutinho.
   Mandevilla burle-marxii Markgraf.
   Merianthera burle-marxii J. Wurdack.
   Microlicia burle-marxii Mello Barreto.
   Neoglaziovia burle-marxii Leme.
   Neoregelia elmoriana Luther.
   Ortophytum burle-marxii L.B. Smith et R.W. Read.
   Ortophytum lymanianum Pereira et Penna.
   Philodendron burle-marxii G.M. Barroso.
   Philodendron grazielae Bunt.
   Philodendron mellobarretoanum Burle Marx ex G.M. Barroso.
   Philodendron pulchrum G.M. Barroso.
   Pitcairnia burle-marxii R. Braga et D. Sucre.
   Pleurostima burle-marxii L.B. Smith.
   Pleurostima fanni N. Menezes.
   Pleurostima piqueteana N. Men. et M. Silva.
   Pontederia burle-marxii Mello Barreto.
   Vellozia burle-marxii L.B. Smith.
   Xerophyta plicata Spreng var. nov.

9. Species that exist in limited geographical areas, in contrast to cosmopolitan species, which grow in many different places.

10. The popular Brazilian name '*quaresmeiras*' comes from the fact that these flowers bloom during Lent ('*Quaresma*').

11. Conversations between Burle Marx and Clarival Valladares, quoted in *43 Anos de Pintura: Roberto Burle Marx* (Belo Horizonte Museum, 1972).

12. Clarival Valladares, *A unidade plastica na obra de Burle Marx* (Rio de Janeiro, 8 Cadernos Brasileiros, 1964).

13. Bruno Zevi, *L'Espresso*, 16 June 1957, Rome.

14. Bruno Zevi, *Architettura paesagistica Brasiliana di Roberto Burle Marx* (Rome, Galeria nationale di arte moderna, 1957).

15. The 'right angle' sums up a tendency manifest in architecture, painting, furniture design and typography stemming from Cubism.

16. Alexander Pope, from a letter to Lord Burlington, 1731, published in *Alexander Pope: Oeuvres Completes* (Paris, Devaux, 1796).

17. J. Benoist-Méchin, *L'homme et ses jardins* (*Man and his Gardens*) (Paris, Albin et Michel, 1975).

18. Name given by Guillaume Apollinaire to the more lyrical branch of Cubism, concerned with light and colour, practised by artists such as Fernand Léger and Robert Delauney.

19. The ha-ha is a ditch with a wall below ground level on its inner side, forming a boundary without obstructing views.

20. Plants that grow without direct contact with the ground, climbing on other plants but without feeding off them. Their roots get water from the humus that collects between them and their support.

Part Two

Gardens

Part Two

Gardens

Rio de Janeiro is the only great city that has managed not to dislodge nature. **PAUL CLAUDEL**

'A garden is the interaction of man and nature, where the right balance between the small interior world and the immensity of the exterior world recreates harmony and achieves serenity.'

Brazil is a country of contrasts, of light and shade, noise and music. Everything clashes: colours, landscapes, races. Poverty and ignorance live side by side with opulence and the most sophisticated technology. The Amazon rainforest, the largest and richest in the world, faces the advance of a desert that encroaches by the day. It is a country of action and passion, nourished by hopes and dreams. All these characteristics are present in the work of Roberto Burle Marx.

He lived in Rio de Janeiro, a city where the landscape is omnipresent. Its huge bay, along a winding coastline, is surrounded by *morros* – granite hills in dramatic and voluptuous formations, some formed of bare rock, some covered with luxuriant vegetation with peaks which abruptly pierce the clouds. They are a ghostly spectacle, especially when the city is bathed in the filtered light of the afternoon sun.

Because of its topography, the city has been built along the shore, between the sea and the mountain. This makes urban development very difficult: its inhabitants have had to excavate tunnels, build an airport out into the sea and construct viaducts and a 15-kilometre-long bridge spanning the bay.

The forest is ubiquitous, its colours intensified by the humidity. The blinding light creates huge contrasts which are accentuated and varied by the speed with which it changes. The atmosphere, a kind of mist, is almost solid, enveloping, sensuous. It is in this environment that Burle Marx created most of his work.

Atlantic rainforest, Itatiaia National Park, Río de Janeiro.

Chapter Four

Public Gardens

'It is through gardens that we add enjoyment to our lives, lives that reflect the ups and downs of industrial civilization. In a garden, people can come into contact with nature, breathe, meditate, observe a flower in a tranquil space. Young people can find sport and entertainment. In an ordered garden with a personality all its own, we can find and recover real time, not the illusory speed dictated by consumer society.'

In Part II of this book I have respected the way that Burle Marx classified his landscapes: public gardens and private gardens. He placed a great deal of emphasis on the difference between the two, stressing the importance of respecting the social function of public works. Community activity provided guidelines very different from those generated by a garden for a specific individual.

To these categories I have added a third. It contains only one example. It is so unique and personal that is incomparable: the garden he made for himself - an enchanted, constantly changing garden, a laboratory of wonders where amazing metamorphoses occurred.

Detail of Burle Marx's drawing for the Praça Arthur Oscar in Recife, 1935.

The Rio de Janeiro Coastline

Over a period of fifty years Burle Marx created
a series of public gardens along the coastline
of Guanabara Bay, as far as the open sea of
the Atlantic. Those at Santos Dumont Airport,
the Museum of Modern Art, the World War II
Memorial, the Parque do Flamengo and the
beaches of Botafogo and Copacabana were
constructed on land reclaimed from the sea,
infilled partly through the removal of the
morro Santo Antônio in the 1950s. The length
of time between the first garden and the last
illustrates the distinct phases through which
Burle Marx's compositions passed.

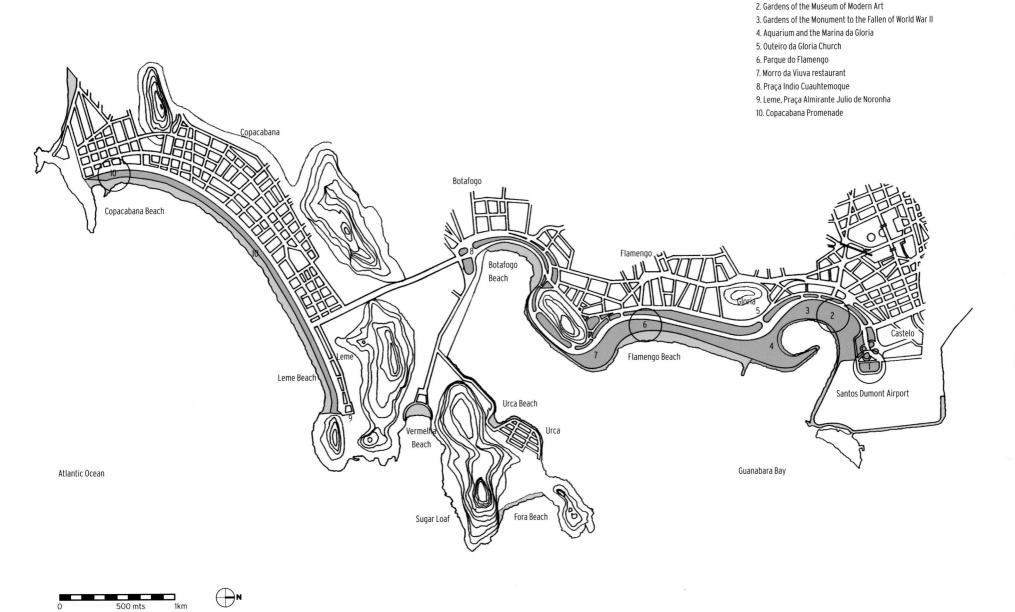

Gardens along the seafront
1. Praça Senador Salgado Filho
2. Gardens of the Museum of Modern Art
3. Gardens of the Monument to the Fallen of World War II
4. Aquarium and the Marina da Gloria
5. Outeiro da Gloria Church
6. Parque do Flamengo
7. Morro da Viuva restaurant
8. Praça Indio Cuauhtemoque
9. Leme, Praça Almirante Julio de Noronha
10. Copacabana Promenade

Copacabana

Copacabana Beach

Botafogo

Botafogo Beach

Flamengo

Gloria

Castelo

Flamengo Beach

Santos Dumont Airport

Leme

Leme Beach

Urca Beach

Urca

Vermelha Beach

Atlantic Ocean

Guanabara Bay

Sugar Loaf

Fora Beach

0   500 mts   1km

N

Praça Senador Salgado Filho

Location Santos Dumont Airport, Rio de Janeiro

Date 1938

Architecture Marcelo, Milton and Mauricio Roberto

Area 13,500m²

Situated in front of Santos Dumont Airport, these gardens are in Burle Marx's undulating, organic style of the late 1930s and 1940s.

The park features a lake containing aquatic plants, with large stones dotted on areas of grass between palm trees, and mainly native vegetation - rubber plants *Ficus retusa,* bougainvilleas *Bougainvillea arborea,* cannonball trees *Couroupita guianensis,* as well as *Clusia fluminensis* and *Cecropia adenopus.* Grouped by species, the vegetation provides dense areas of shade which give way to contrasting luminous areas. Cement benches, several metres in length, snake along beside the paths.

The airport is one of the gateways to the city, so the gardens greet the new arrival with a vision of a mysterious, secluded universe, far removed from the hustle and bustle of urban life.

Original plan by Burle Marx.

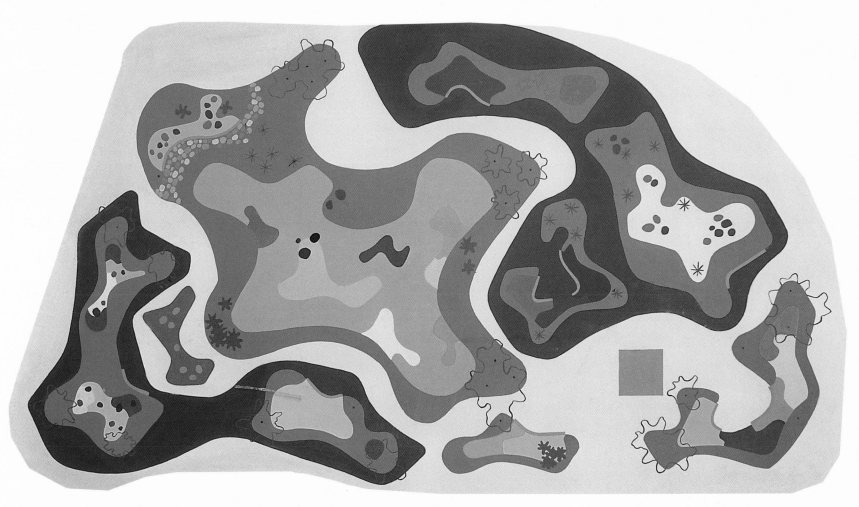

Plant List (partial)

Anacardium occidentale L.
Arecastrum romanzoffianum (Cham) Becc.
Basiloxylon brasiliensis (Fr. All).
Canna sp.
Cecropia adenopus Mart.
Cecropia hololeuca Miq.
Chorisia crispiflora H.B.K.
Clusia fluminensis Pl. et Triana.
Coccos nucifera L.
Cyrtopodium andersonii R-Br.

Dichorisandra thyrsiflora Mikan.
Ficus nymphaefolia Mill.
Ficus retusa L.
Joannesia princeps Vell.
Montrichardia linifera Schott.
Nymphaea capensis Thunb. var. Zanzibariensis, Casp.
Philodendron undulatum Engl.
Tibouchina sp.
Vellozia plicata Mart.
Victoria regia Lindl.

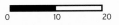

0   10   20

N

[left] One of the long, curving concrete benches, shown shortly after the garden was completed.

[opposite] Stones dot the grass beneath the palm trees.

Parque do Flamengo (now Parque Brigadeiro Eduardo Gomes)

Location   Aterro Gloria-Flamengo,[1] Rio de Janeiro

Date   1961-65

Architecture   Affonso Reidy, Jorge Machado Moreira,
Carlos Werneck de Carvalho, Helio Mamede

Engineering   Berta Leitchic

Botany   Luiz Emyglio de Mello

Landscape architecture   Roberto Burle Marx

Area   1,200,000m²

This project came about in order solve a traffic problem. The scheme had to provide a highway on a narrow stretch of coast between the hills and the sea. The plan was designed by a working group of botanists, engineers and architects and envisaged not only a two-speed highway with pedestrian crossings at various levels but also areas designated for cultural and recreational activities. These included stages for music and theatre, tree-lined car parks, areas for picnicking, relaxing and playing games, restaurants and an aquarium, as well as a big sports infrastructure providing basketball, volleyball and tennis courts, spaces for flying model aircraft and a marina for boats and fishing.

Built on reclaimed land, the park had to form a transition area between the sea, the city and the mountains. The team responsible for the project decided that it should go right down to the sea, emulating the sinuous contours of Guanabara Bay. By moulding the ground into different levels it was possible to isolate the park visually and acoustically from the main road and separate the different activities from each other. Ironically, many motorists have lamented the fact they have lost their view of the sea.

The careful sculpting of the terrain produces such varied environments that walking round the park becomes a real adventure. The rest areas are intimate enclaves set into hollows

Drawing based on the original plan.

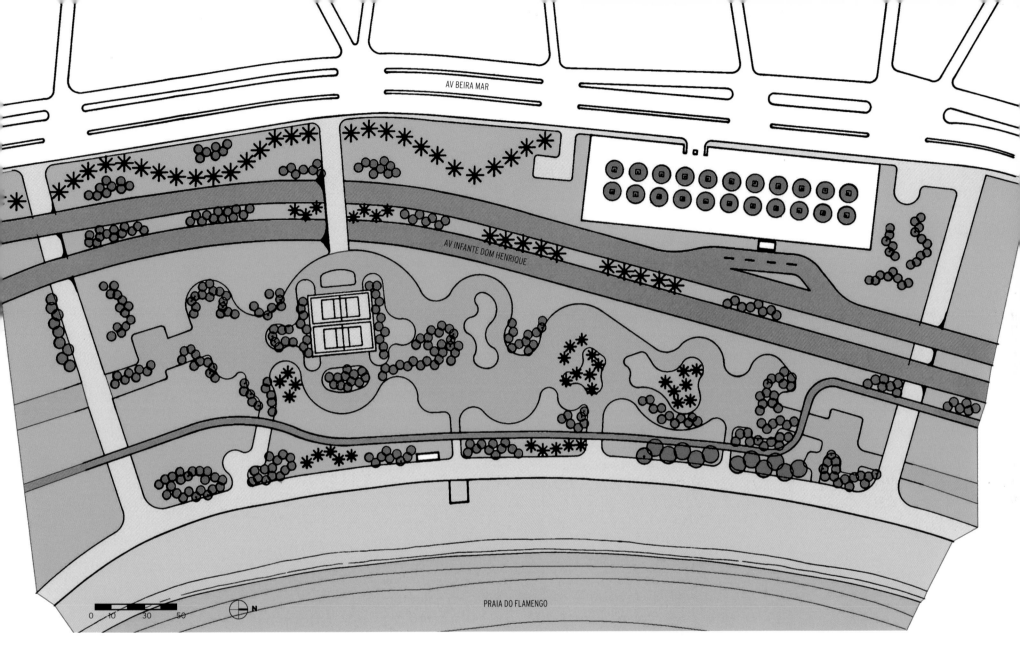

AV BEIRA MAR

AV INFANTE DOM HENRIQUE

PRAIA DO FLAMENGO

0   10   30   50   ⊕ N

Plant List (partial)

Allamanda cathartica L.
Anthurium coriaceum (Gran.) Engl.
Arecastrum romanzoffianum (Cham.) Becc.
Bombax ceiba L.
Bombax malabaricum DC.
Brunfelsia grandiflora D. Don.
Bumelia obtusifolia Roem. et Schult.
Caesalpinia echinata Lam.
Caesalpinia ferrea Mart.

Caesalpinia peltophoroides Benth.
Cassia multijuga A. Rich.
Ceiba erianthos K. Schum.
Chorisia crispiflora H.B.K.
Chrysalidocarpus lucubensis Becc.
Clusia fluminensis Pl. et Triana.
Clusia rosea Jacq. Enum.
Cocos nucifera L.
Couroupita guianensis Aubl.

Delonix regia (Boj.) Raf.
Diplothemium maritimum Mart.
Dracaena arborea Hort.
Enterolobium contortisiliquum Rauman.
Erythrina falcata Benth.
Euterpe oleracea Mart.
Furcraea gigantea Vent.
Lagerstroemia speciosa Pers.
Latania commersonii Gmell.

Mimusops coriacea Miq.
Nolina recurvata Hemsl.
Pennisetum villosum Br.
Philodendron bipinatifidum Schott.
Philodendron mellobarretoanum Burle Marx
    ex G.M. Barroso
Pithecolobium tortum Mart.
Plumeria alba L.
Rapanea guianensis Aubl.

Roystonia regia O.F. Cook L.C.
Schizolobium parahybum (Vell.) Blake.
Stenotaphrum americanum Schrank.
Stenotaphrum americanum (Schrank) variegata
    Hort.
Syagrus comosa Mart.
Tibouchina corymbosa (Raddi) Cogn.
Tibouchina radula Mgf.
Washingtonia filifera Wendl.

67

protected from the wind and sea by clumps of thick bushes and shady trees along the paths. The zone nearest the sea slopes evenly down to an artificial beach where rows of palm trees punctuate the space and mark a boundary while allowing a clear view of the bay beyond their slender trunks.

Visitors do not come to the Parque do Flamengo to escape the city, to dream and lose themselves in nature. They come for the specific activities, which they can enjoy in a natural environment. Because of the huge number of people who flood into these gardens at the weekends – more than 150,000 – one of the lanes of the highway is closed on Sundays allowing walkers and cyclists to circulate unhindered by traffic. With a view to providing a little train to travel the long distances between the different activity areas, one of the pedestrian paths was paved in concrete; it is now used for jogging. Pedestrian bridges over the highway and underpasses below have gentle slopes and enough light for people to feel comfortable using them.

The plant selection was based on blocks of the same species arranged in a harmonious balance of solids and voids, placed in some cases to be seen from passing cars. There are so many different species of palms that together they constitute a valuable collection. Colour is brought to the park by the trees which bloom at different times of the year, rather than by costly and high-maintenance flower beds. They include floss-silk trees *Chorisia speciosa, Bombax malabaricum,* queen's flower *Lagerstroemia flos-reginae, Acacia seyal,* false silk cotton trees *Pseudobombax ellipticum,* orchids *Bauhinia blakeana* and cannonball trees *Couroupita guianensis.*

A prime example of a large-scale urban garden, the Parque do Flamengo was a controversial project. One criticism was that it lacked flower beds. Another was that, for a tropical country, there was not enough shade. The Praça Senador Salgado Filho, with its leafy trees, clearly shows what Burle Marx's more recent gardens will be like when they reach maturity. Among the critics were doubtless those who wanted to occupy this large empty space. Fortunately it is now protected and declared an area of national heritage.

[left] Aerial view of the area for flying model aircraft, the highway and two pedestrian bridges at the time of construction.

[far left] A mass of *Bombax malabaricum*.

[left] Coconut trees along the beach with the Sugar Loaf in the distance.

[far left] View of Igreja da Gloria, showing a pedestrian bridge over the highway, with a group of palms *Butia capitata* and *Ficus elastica*.

[left] Fast lane of the lower highway.

[opposite] Aerial view of Praça Indio Cuauhtemoque, Botafogo, an area of the Parque do Flamengo.

Location Parque do Flamengo, Rio de Janeiro

Date 1954

Architecture Affonso Reidy

Area 60,000m²

The Museum of Modern Art occupies pride of place in the Aterro Gloria-Flamengo. Burle Marx's landscape design complements the building's Rationalist architecture. Perpendicular forms of beds frame monochrome patches of plants – some delicate and feathery in texture, others stiff and lance-like – and areas of smooth or rough stones, creating contrasts of texture and colour. The gardens envelop the building, sometimes penetrating it in courtyards and terraces, and covering its roof. This building-garden dialogue is the result of a continual exchange of ideas between the architect and landscape designer.

[left] Roberto Burle Marx watching the construction of the gardens.

[opposite] Drawing based on the original plan.

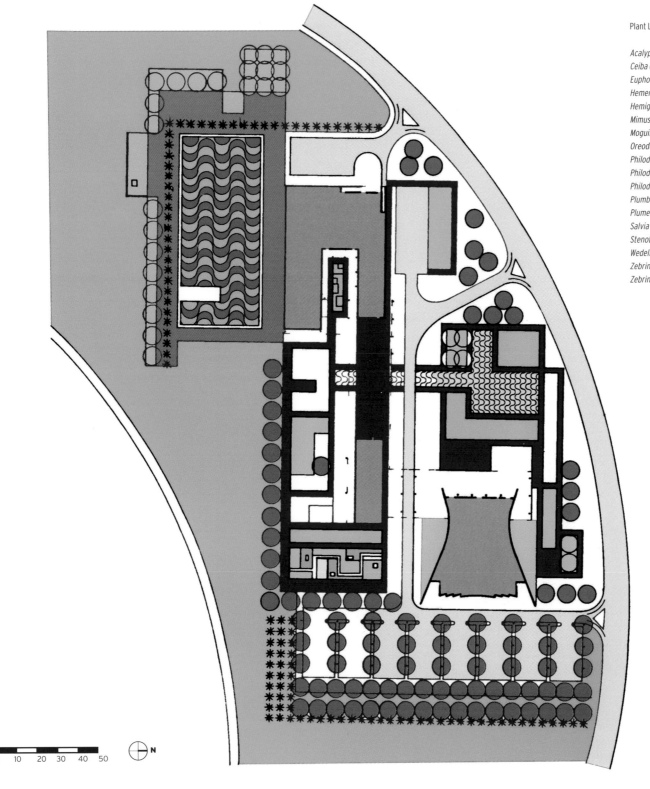

Plant List (partial)

Acalypha wilkesiana DC. var. musaica Hort.
Ceiba erianthos K. Schum
Euphorbia splendens B.D.J.
Hemerocallis flava L.
Hemigraphis colorata Hallier.
Mimusops coriacea Mik.
Moguilea tomentosa Benth.
Oreodoxa oleracea Mart.
Philodendron mellobarretoanum Burle Marx ex G.M. Barroso.
Philodendron myrmecophyllum Engl.
Philodendron selloum K. Koch.
Plumbago capensis Thunb.
Plumeria alba L.
Salvia splendens Sellow.
Stenotaphrum americanum (Schrank) var. variegata, Hort.
Wedelia paludosa DC. var. vialis DC.
Zebrina pendula Schnitzlein.
Zebrina purpusii Brueckner.

0 10 20 30 40 50

N

[left] The roof garden with courtyard in the foreground.

[left] The sculpture garden for open-air exhibitions with *Ficus elastica* in the background.

[opposite] An arrangement of river boulders and blocks of granite rescued from house demolitions, with *Clusia fluminensis* behind.

Copacabana Promenade

Location   Copacabana Beach, Rio de Janeiro

Date   1970

Length   4km

Old photographs of Copacabana show a neighbourhood of houses and gardens. Over the years, a wall of buildings has been constructed reaching right down to the sea, confirming Le Corbusier's prediction: 'You are going to build a wall of egoists!'

In order to create a transition area for vehicles and pedestrian traffic between the sea and the city, land was reclaimed from the sea and a thoroughfare was constructed. Physical constraints affecting Copacabana (entrances to car parks and underground service installations) restricted the depth of the landscaping project, so the solution adopted was an open, broad pavement with groups of trees planted where the services allowed sufficient depth. The pavement was constructed in Portuguese stone mosaic, a medium which allows thermal expansion and has become traditional in Rio. Its design in black, white and red was conceived so that it could be seen in its entirety from the tops of nearby buildings and in detail by passing motorists, pedestrians and customers in the cafés.

For the walkway beside the beach, Burle Marx reproduced a traditional Portuguese design of black and white parabolic waves, which had become the famous trademark of the beaches at Copacabana. Sea-breeze-resistant vegetation is dotted here and there to provide shade for benches. Coconut palms, characteristic of the coast, evoke the languor of a seaside resort.

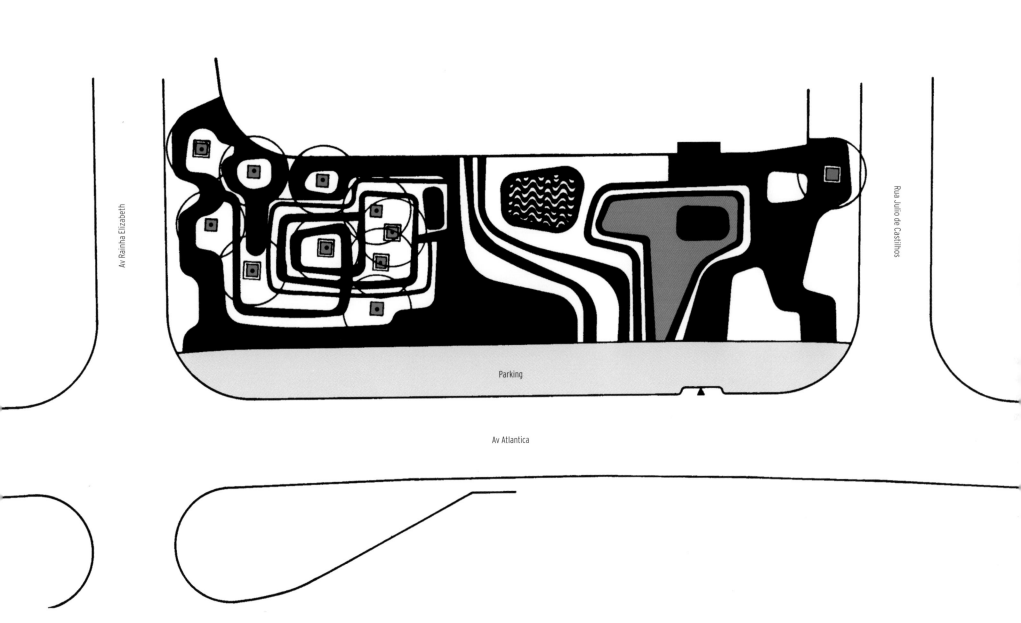

Av Rainha Elizabeth

Rua Julio de Castilhos

Parking

Av Atlantica

Detail based on the original plan.

0   5   10   15   20

N

[left] The Copacabana Promenade, stretching four kilometres along the Rio coast.

[opposite] Aerial view showing the distinctive pavement mosaics and the sea-breeze resistant vegetation – *Cocos nucifera, Paritium tiliaceum, Mimusops coriacea, Clusia fluminensis, Coccoloba wiffera, Ficus* and *Terminalia catappa.*

The Centre of Rio

The removal of the *morro* Santo Antônio
left 30 hectares of land in the most valuable
area of Rio free for development. Burle Marx
was asked to create designs for the gardens
of three new skyscrapers (Petrobras, BNDES
and the Bank of Brazil) and for the Santa
Tereza Tram Terminal, the Convent of
Santo Antônio and the Metropolitan Cathedral.
He also designed the Largo da Carioca,
a large square catering for a huge volume
of pedestrian traffic. The result is extremely
harmonious and makes this part of the city
an important achievement in terms
of urban planning.

1. Petrobras Building
2. Santa Tereza Tram Terminal
3. National Economic and Social Development Bank Building (BNDES)
4. Largo da Carioca
5. Bank of Brazil
6. Metropolitan Cathedral
7. Convent of Santo Antônio

Petrobras Building

Location   Rio de Janeiro

Date   1969

Architecture   José María Gandolfi, Luiz Forte Neto,

Roberto Gandolfi, Vicente Ferreira de Castro,

José Sanchotene and Abrão Anizassad

Area of ground-level gardens   6,300m²

Area of terraces   1,000m² each

The landscape design for the twenty-five-storey Petrobras tower comprises open ground-level areas around the building and twelve terraces ranged up the height of the tower facing the four cardinal points.

From within, the ground-level garden appears as a composition of predominantly green textures that reproduces the architectural language. Horizontal planes of water, stone and vegetation criss-cross each other in a regular woven pattern and create a sense of calm in the boiling cauldron of the city around them.

Walking through the garden, the sound and sparkle of the waterfalls produces a more dynamic rhythm. The difference in level between the plaza and the sloping street below is resolved by a cement *bas-relief*.

The terraces are two or three floors high and all have different designs. Some contain tanks of emergency fire water disguised in a central planter. Others, liberated from this function, have patterned stone floors and planted borders. The plants selected are resistant to winds blowing at this height.

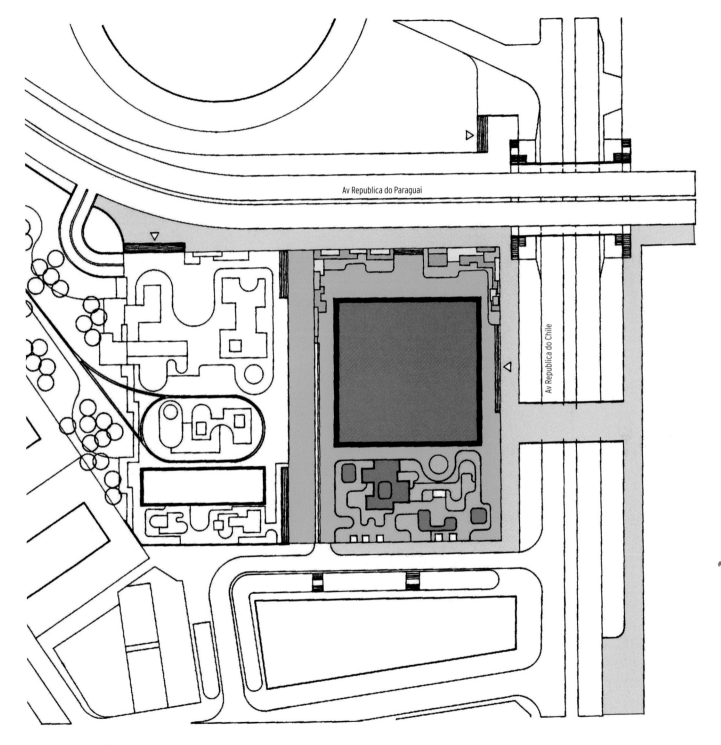

Plant List (partial)

Ground floor
Calathea litzei E. Morr.
Cassia bicapsularis L.
Hemerocallis flava L.
Nelumbo nucifera Gaertn. (pink).
Philodendron latilobum Schott.
Philodendron myrmecophyllum Engl.
Plumbago capensis Thunb.
Tibouchina trichopoda Baill.

East façade
Anthurium andreanum Linden.
Ophiopogon japonicus Ker.-Gawl.
Philodendron corcovadense Kunth. Enum.
Xanthosoma violaceum Schott.
Zebrina purpusii Bruekner.

North façade
Aechmea fasciata Baker.
Calathea orbiculata Lodd.
Clusia hilairiana Schlecht.
Monstera deliciosa Liebm.
Philodendron burle-marxii G.M. Barroso.
Schizocasia Lauterbachiana Engl.
Streptocalyx floribunda.
Vriesia imperialis E. Morr.

West façade
Clusia fluminensis Pl. et Triana.
Philodendron maximum Krause.
Philodendron wilsonii.
Solanum violaefolium Schott.
Zebrina purpusii Brueckner.

South façade
Brassaia actinophylla F. Muell.
Jatropha podagrica Hook.
Monstera friedrischsthalii Shot.
Nolina recurvata Hemsl.
Philodendron pittieri Engl.

Av Republica do Paraguai

Av Republica do Chile

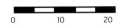

0   10   20

 N

Drawing based on the original plan.

[far left] Aerial view of the ground-floor garden and concrete *bas-relief*.

[left] Beds of river boulders with *Clusia fluminensis, Philodendron bipinnatifidum* and *Hemerocallis flava*.

[left] One of the double-height covered terraces with patterned floor and a border of *Clusia fluminensis, Philodendron bipinnatifidum, Coccoloba urifero* and *Yucca aloifolia*.

[left] A terrace with a central planter containing *Brassaia actinophylla* concealing a water tank.

Santa Tereza Tram Terminal
(now Praça Monsenhor Francisco Pinto)

Location Rio de Janeiro

Date 1972

Architecture Flavio Marinho do Rego and Paulo Conde

Area 21,700m²

Underground parking for the Petrobras Building was constructed on adjoining land belonging to Santa Tereza Tram Terminal. Burle Marx created a garden on the roof of the car park, merging with the ground-level garden of the Petrobras tower. Like its neighbour, the Tram Terminal garden is an elaborate composition based on the theme of the urban grid, playing positive against negative. Ventilation ducts are hidden inside planters surrounded by bushes and climbing plants. A lawn is planted with grasses of different textures and the pavement has geometric mosaic patterns of Portuguese stone in contrasting colours.

Drawing based on the original plan.

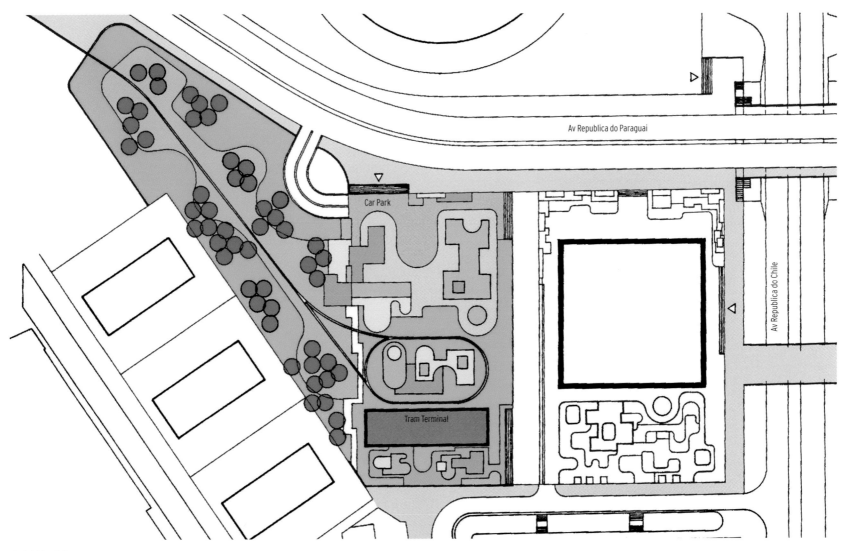

Av Republica do Paraguai

Car Park

Tram Terminal

Av Republica do Chile

Plant List (partial)

Allamanda cathartica L. var. nobilis.
Allamanda purpurea Gard.
Anthurium coriaceum G. Don.
Bauhinia blakeana Dunn.
Brassaia actinophylla F. Muell.
Cassia bicapsularis L.
Ceiba erianthos K. Schum.
Chorisia speciosa St. Hil.
Clusia fluminensis Pl. et Triana.

Clusia hilairiana Schlecht.
Clusia sp. (de Pedra Azul).
Coccoloba uvifera L.
Congea tomentosa Roxb.
Cortaderia selloana Aschers et Graebn.
Crinum asiaticum L.
Furcraea gigantea Vent.
Jatropha podagrica Hook.
Moquilea tomentosa Benth.

Ouratea cuspidata Engl.
Philodendron bipinnatifidum Schott.
Philodendron mellobarretoanum
    Burle Marx ex G.M. Barroso.
Plumbago capensis Thunb.
Thunbergia erecta T. Anders.
Tibouchina corymbosa Cogn.
Wedelia paludosa DC. var. vialis, DC.
Yucca aloifolia L.

0   10   20

N

[left] The varying green textures
of *Allamanda cathartica*, *Crinum asiaticum*,
Agave angustifolia 'marginata', *Wedelia
paludosa* and *Congea tomentosa*.

[opposite] On the roof of the underground
car park, planters of different heights, which
conceal air vents, contain *Setcreasea purpurea*
and *Plumbago capensis*, surrounded by a
patterned floor of Portuguese stone.

National Economic and Social Development Bank (BNDES)

Location Rio de Janeiro

Dates 1974 and 1985

Architecture Alfredo Willer, Ariel Steele, Joel Ramalho Jr,

José Sanchotene, Leonardo Oba, Rubens Sanchotene and Oscar Müller

Area 7,300m²

The BNDES faces the Petrobras Building, with a pedestrian walkway connecting the two at their front access level over the major artery road, Republica do Chile Avenue. Part of the *morro* Santo Antônio was removed to build the company's car park, and once the work was finished a garden was conceived which would recreate the primitive form of the hill. Because the garden rises in a steep slope over a concrete mound, there is a constant threat that frequent heavy rain will erode the soil. A solution was found in ground-cover plants, with roots that help to stabilize the earth.

The colours and textures of the plant selection and the open courtyards dug out of the bank can be clearly seen from the top floors of the tower. The plants covering the sloping land are arranged in large free-form masses, with greenery tumbling over into the sunken courtyards, which are like cloisters isolated from the urban hustle and bustle. Sitting there, you can hear the murmur of water and only just make out the silhouette of the buildings in the background.

The Convent of Santo Antônio asked Burle Marx to redesign its adjacent garden to merge with that of BNDES. Sadly, today it has to be protected from delinquency behind railings and walls.

Drawing based on the original plan.

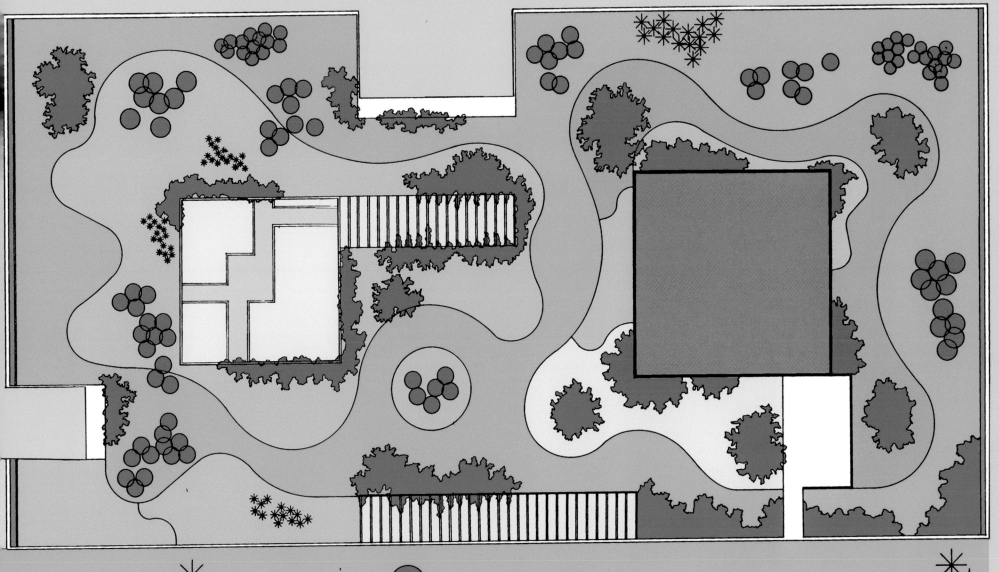

Plant List (partial)

Allamanda cathartica L.

Beloperone guttata
    T. S. Brandegge.

Bougainvillea aurantiaca Hort.

Bougainvillea spectabilis Willd.

Cassia alata L.

Clusia fluminensis Pl. et Triana.

Clusia sp.

Coccoloba uvifera L.

Congea tomentosa Roxb.

Costus spiralis Roec.

Furcraea gigantea Vent.

Hemerocallis fulva L.

Monstera deliciosa Liebm.

Philodendron bipinnatifidum
    Schott.

Plumbago capensis Thunb.

Plumeria alba L.

Thunbergia grandiflora Roxb.

Vriesia imperialis Carrière.

Xanthosoma violaceum Schott.

Zebrina pendula Schnizl.

0   10   20

N

[left] The soil on the sloping site is preserved with large beds of ground-covering plants mixed with *Congea tomentosa* and *Furcraea gigantea*.

[left] *Philodendron wilsonii*, *Philodendron bipinnatifidum* and *Allamanda cathartica* drape into a sunken garden. On the columns are *Dracaena marginata* and *Dracaena fragans*.

[opposite] The view from the tower shows the unity of the design, integrating the ventilation shafts of the car park and sunken courtyards planted with *Yucca gloriosa*, *Vriesia imperialis* and *Hemerocallis flava*.

Largo da Carioca

Location Rio de Janeiro

Dates 1981 and 1985

Area 2 hectares

The Largo da Carioca is a giant abstract picture designed to be viewed from the surrounding buildings. It acts as a focal point for all the converging gardens in the area. The design was worked around elements already in the square - a fountain, a clock tower, ventilation ducts - using red, white and black Portuguese stone, grass and water. Four years after the square was completed, renovation work began on the subway train system below, and the square had to be completely rebuilt in a slightly modified form. The aquatic element no longer exists because it was impossible to keep the water clean in a public area as crowded as the centre of Rio.

Original plan by Burle Marx.

[left] Detail of the plan.

[left] The Convent of Santo Antônio and part of the Largo da Carioca.

[opposite] The square is an intersection for heavy pedestrian traffic and forms a hub of open space in the city for vendors and street artists.

Bank of Brazil

Location Cidade de São Sebastião do Rio de Janiero Building, Rio de Janeiro
Date 1968
Architecture Marcello Graça Couto Campello
Area 1,240m²

Adjoining the complex of gardens in the centre of Rio, the Bank of Brazil built an exterior garden that gives onto the Rua Senador Dantas, which is old, narrow and extremely busy with very limited views. The design was conceived around verticality. Specially built metal columns covered with moss, bark and plants tower over passers-by. The garden is complemented by patterns in the pavement.

Metropolitan Cathedral

Location Rio de Janeiro
Date 1968
Architecture Luiz Fabricio Menescal

At the Metropolitan Cathedral, a large mass of bauhinia orchids *Bauhinia blakeana* climbs the sides of the steps to the main entrance in staggered planters. This is the only part of the scheme to have been realized. In the original design, however, pools ringed by benches and patterns on the paving of the esplanade echoed the circular shape of the cathedral. Unfortunately this area is currently used as a public car park.

Drawing of the Metropolitan Cathedral
based on the original plan.

Plant List (partial)

Bauhinia blakeana Dunn.
Caesalpinia ferrea Mart.
Caesalpinia peltophoroides Benth.
Canna indica L.(red).
Couroupita guianensis Aubl.
Cyperus giganteus Vahl.
Erythrina falcata Benth.
Hemerocallis flava L.
Nymphaea capensis Thunb. var. zanzibariensis, Casp.
Philodendron speciosum Schott.

0 10 20 30 40 50

N

Secret Gardens

With the construction of skyscrapers,
verticality has become the dominant feature
in the modern city. Burle Marx's response
was to make gardens vertical too, constructing
them on the surface of walls, designing them
to be seen from above, converting roofs
into gardens and inventing solutions for
planting in shallow earth.

Drawing by Burle Marx of the Brazilian Pavilion by architect
Sergio Bernardez at the Brussels International Fair, 1958.

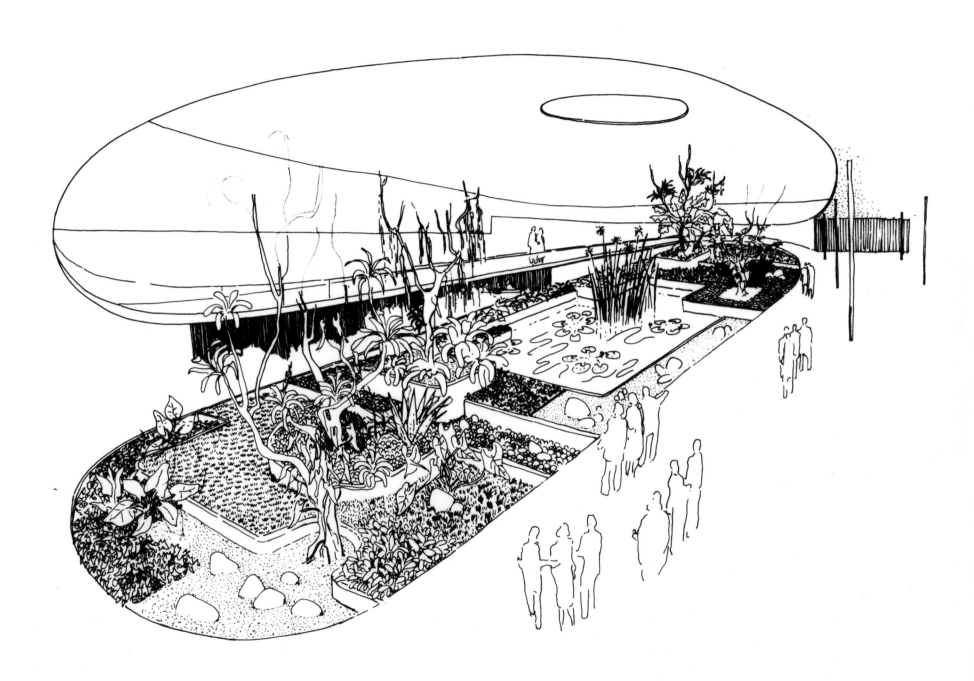

Rio Business Centre: Argentina Building and 9 de Julho Car Park

Location   Rio de Janeiro

Date   1981

Architecture   Claudio Fortes and Roberto Victor

Area   2,300m²

When the capital of Brazil was moved to Brasilia, the old house occupied by the Argentine Embassy was abandoned and eventually pulled down. Two towers were built in its place: one a twenty-seven-floor office building and the other a fifteen-storey car park. The new design preserves the old garden's imperial palms *Roystonea regia* – now grown to a height of 30 metres – and hundred-year-old rubber plants *Ficus microcarpa*. Around these original elements Burle Marx created a garden full of subtlety. Set below ground level and surrounded by low walls overrun with flowing water and plants, the atmosphere of this sunken garden is one of intimacy, despite the continual flow of pedestrians. For anyone walking through, it is an oasis.

[left] The garden of palm trees is sunk below the level of the busy pavement alongside, with hundred-year-old *Ficus microcarpa* emerging from the transparent architecture.

[opposite] Drawing based on the original plan.

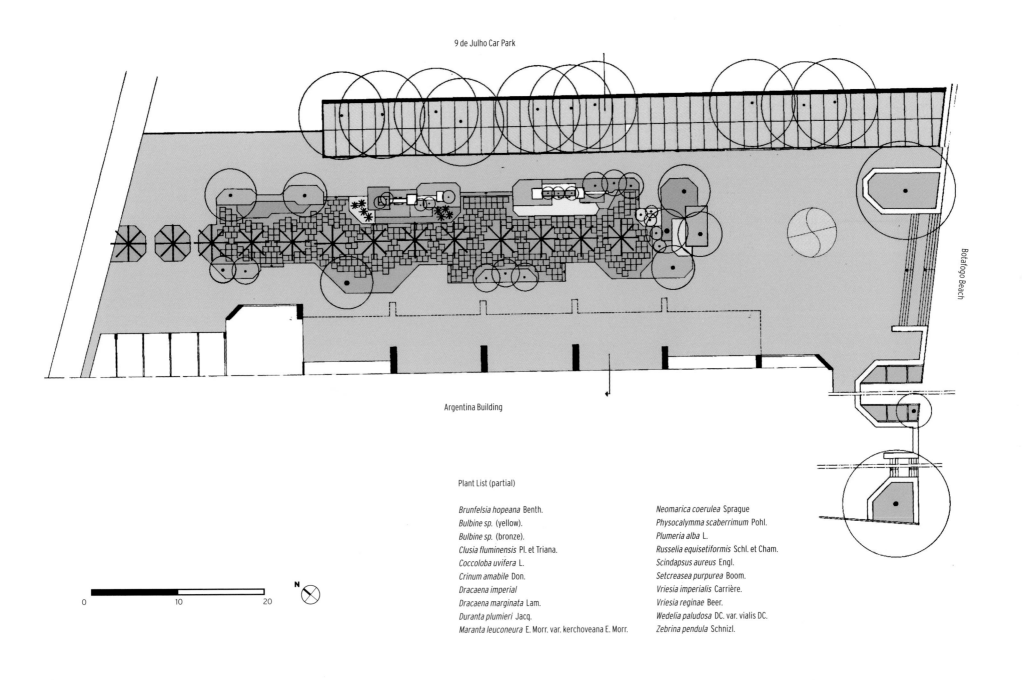

9 de Julho Car Park

Botafogo Beach

Argentina Building

0   10   20

N

Plant List (partial)

Brunfelsia hopeana Benth.
Bulbine sp. (yellow).
Bulbine sp. (bronze).
Clusia fluminensis Pl. et Triana.
Coccoloba uvifera L.
Crinum amabile Don.
Dracaena imperial
Dracaena marginata Lam.
Duranta plumieri Jacq.
Maranta leuconeura E. Morr. var. kerchoveana E. Morr.

Neomarica coerulea Sprague
Physocalymma scaberrimum Pohl.
Plumeria alba L.
Russelia equisetiformis Schl. et Cham.
Scindapsus aureus Engl.
Setcreasea purpurea Boom.
Vriesia imperialis Carrière.
Vriesia reginae Beer.
Wedelia paludosa DC. var. vialis DC.
Zebrina pendula Schnizl.

[left] *Scindapsus aureus* and *Philodendron* climb the imperial palms, modifying their slender silhouettes.

[opposite] The central body of plants is characterized by creepers and the aerial roots of *Ficus elastica*, creating an intimate, calm environment.

Xerox Brazil Building

Location   Rio de Janeiro

Dates   1980-82

Architecture   Pontual Associates and Planeamiento Ltda.

Interior design   Janete Ferreira da Costa

In renovating a four-storey warehouse for Xerox Brazil, the architects created a central courtyard covered by a translucent roof to bring natural light into all the offices. The ingenuity of the landscaping lay in erecting a sophisticated metal structure that trailed plants up past the windows of every floor. The armature was covered in spongy bark, 'xaxim', so that the roots of epiphytes – a variety of bromeliads, orchids and anthuriums – could cling and climb the framework. The composition is an impressive sight, transforming the central space into a mass of green light. On the ground floor Burle Marx worked with rough stones and other textures, contrasting them with black polished granite and water.

[left] The courtyard at ground-floor level, where a dining area is located.

[opposite] Preliminary sketch by Burle Marx.

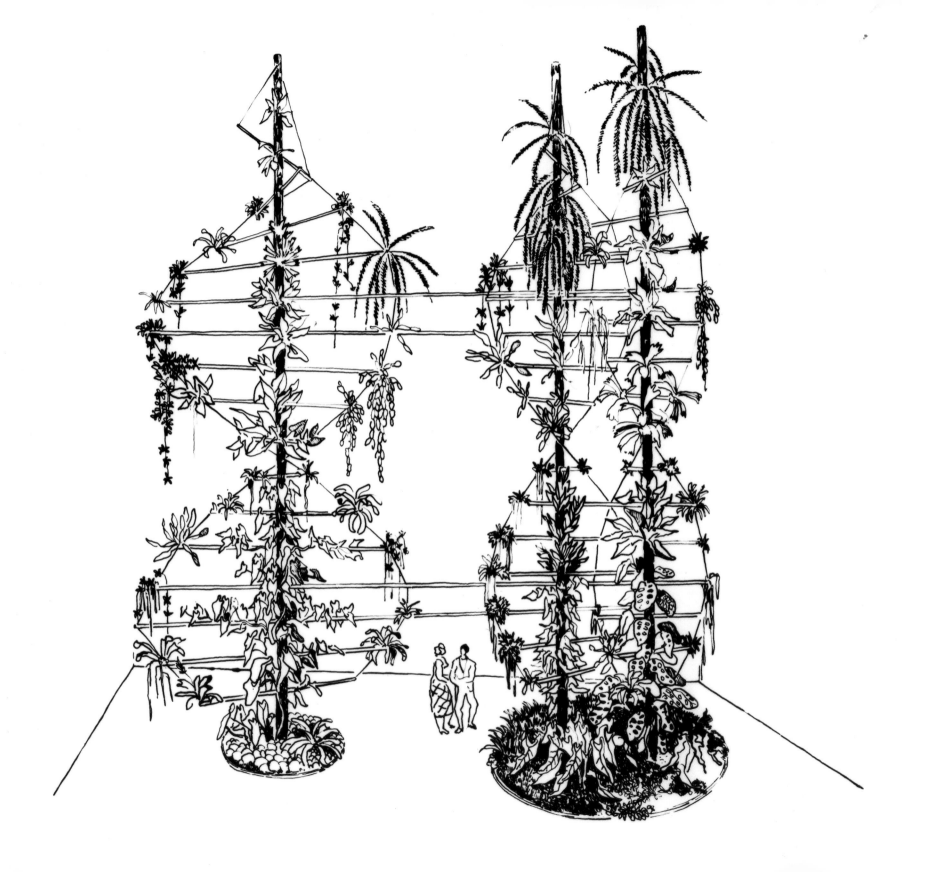

[left] View of the central atrium from a fourth-floor office.

[left] Worm's-eye view showing *Philodendron hastatum* climbing one of the bark-covered metal columns.

[opposite] A 'green column' of epiphytes – *Philodendron lalilobum, Philodendron wilsonii, Neoregelia compacta* and *Polypodium aureum.*

CAEMI Foundation

Location Rio de Janeiro

Date 1984

Architecture Edson and Edmundo Musa

Area 1,500m²

As well as designing the terraces and courtyards of the CAEMI Foundation, Burle Marx extended the mosaic floor of the entrance plaza out onto the pavement around the building. The geometrical design was executed in granite and Portuguese stone in three colours.

Alongside the mosaic were placed borders with plants of highly contrasting textures and shapes.

This unusual project, integrating the building and the pavement, invites in passers-by - an approach that could be seen as something of a marketing exercise.

Drawing based on the original plan.

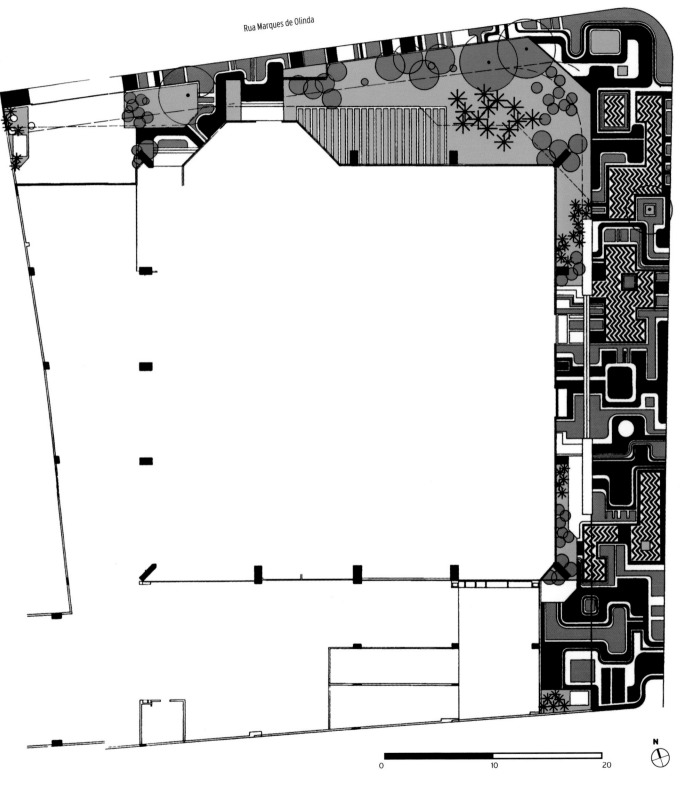

Rua Marques de Olinda

Av Botafogo Beach

Plant List (partial)

Anthurium coriaceum G. Don.
Anthurium plowmanii Croat.
Asparagus sprengeri Regel.
Bauhinia blakeana Dunn.
Clusia fluminensis Pl. et Triana.
Clusia sp. (de Pedra Azul).
Crinum amabile Don.
Crinum sp. (white).
Dracaena marginata Lam.
Ficus lyrata Warb.
Hemigraphis sp. (Honolulu).
Licuala grandis H. Wendl.
Megaskepasma erythrochlamys Lindau.
Neoregelia compacta (Mez.) L. B. Smith.
Ophiopogun japonicus Ker.-Gawl.
Philodendron martianum Engl.
Philodendron mellobarretoanum
    Burle Marx ex G. M. Barroso.
Philodendron wilsonii.
Pinanga kuhlii Blume.
Pleomele reflexa N. E. Brown.
Plumeria alba L.
Russelia equisetiformis Cham. et Schlecht.
Schefflera aboricora Hayata.
Schizocentron elegans Meissn.
Scindapsus aureus Engl.
Spathiphyllum cannaefolium Schott.
Thunbergia erecta T. Anders.
Turnera ulmifolia L.
Vriesia imperialis Carrière.
Vriesia reginae Beer.

0   10   20

N

[left] The view from the president of CAEMI's office, with a terrace designed by Burle Marx in the foreground.

[opposite] The mosaic floor of the entrance plaza (to the right) in red, white, grey and black stone was continued out onto the surrounding pavement.

Souza Aguiar Hospital

Location Rio de Janeiro

Date 1966

Architecture Ary García Roza

External mural 12 x 36m

Internal mural 3.5 x 16.5m

This hospital faces one of Rio's largest green spaces – the Campo de Santana. Burle Marx decided, therefore, not to make a traditional garden but to reflect the park opposite.

On the outside wall of the main entrance he created a vertical garden, where planters are arranged in an interplay of receding and protruding volumes with hanging plants and waterfalls. Silhouettes of Rio can be seen through punctures in the wall, bringing the city into the garden. Burle Marx was the first modern exponent of the vertical garden, a 'Burlesque-Marxist' version of the hanging gardens of Babylon.

Inside the building is an impressive mural, made entirely of stones: black basalt and white and red limestone alternate with Brazilian semi-precious stones such as white and pink quartz and amethyst.

[far left] The exterior wall garden with concrete planters containing *Clusia fluminensis, Philodendron bipinnatifidum, Scindapsus aureus* and *Monstera.*

[left] The interior mural made of basalt, limestone and semi-precious stones.

[opposite] Preliminary sketch (above) and scale drawing (below) of the interior mural.

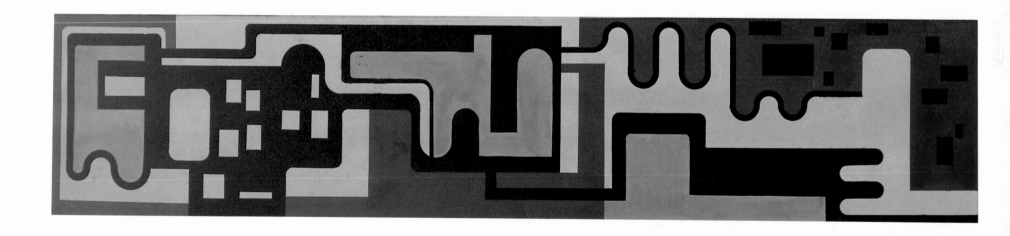

Safra Bank Headquarters

Location São Paulo

Date 1983-88

Architecture Mauricio Kogan

Area of reception floor 1,700m²

Area of roof terrace 1,200m²

Mural 7 x 18m

The Safra Bank Headquarters features two bold designs by Burle Marx: the floor of a large reception room and a roof terrace on top of the complex's lower tower.

The reception floor features a geometric pattern combining carpeted areas and marble in beige, white, red and black. At one end of the room, a moulded concrete relief panel covers a whole wall.

The exterior roof terrace is on the eighth floor. Its formal treatment follows the same theme as the roof garden of the Ministry of Education and Health, which Burle Marx designed in 1938. In the plan for the original project (see page 39), the coloured forms were an abstract representation of the selected flowers. In the completed garden, however, the colours did not correspond to the drawing because the flowers bloom at different times of year. The inclusion of mineral materials on the Safra Bank terrace maintains and accentuates the contrast of colours all the year round, so that the garden appears exactly as it was on paper. The winding paths are made of Portuguese stone in three colours, small boulders are arranged in undulating volumes and the plants are placed in pots hidden under mounds of clay pebbles.

[far left] The lobby floor with its geometric pattern of carpet and stone in black, beige, red and white.

[left] View of the lobby with the concrete relief panel by Burle Marx and Haruyoshi Ono in the background.

[opposite] The roof-terrace floor punctuated with scattered boulders and pebbles.

Brasilia: Where the Sky is the Sea

Throughout Brazilian history, urbanization has spread exclusively along the coast. Its capital cities, Salvador da Bahia and Rio de Janeiro, were no exception. In the 1950s, however, the foresight and determination of President Juscelino Kubitschek brought to fruition an idea that had been around since the seventeenth century. He set the challenge of transferring the capital from Rio to the country's uninhabited centre. First prize in the competition for a pilot design for the new capital was awarded to Lúcio Costa in 1957.

Brasilia was inaugurated in 1960. It was originally meant to house 500,000 inhabitants. Thirty years later the capital and its satellite cities had a population of 1,500,000. Like the new city of Chandigarh in India, designed by Le Corbusier in 1951, Brasilia followed the recommendations of the 1933 Charter of Athens: clearly defined administrative and residential zones; sports facilities; multi-speed thoroughfares for cars and buses and paths for pedestrians; open spaces at ground level and so on.

The theoretical proposal was based, according to Costa, on the 'first gesture anyone makes when taking possession of a site: the sign of the cross',[2] that is, two axes crossing. One axis is designated the government area, the other the residential area, and the point at which they cross is the social zone of commercial and cultural facilities.

The power of the state is expressed in the government axis through the old technique of large monumental embankments, which eliminate the natural unevenness of the terrain. The residential axis is without continuity, each sector existing in its own terms as an autonomous visual organism, creating smaller spaces on a human scale. The impression pursued was one of spaciousness – the distances between the vertical planes of the buildings creating generous horizontal planes – and the legibility and clarity that come from rational planning.

Burle Marx's garden designs for Brasilia had to take into account many factors, including that of a unique landscape. The city is situated on a plateau at an altitude of 800 metres. The horizon and the sky are important elements: Lúcio Costa used to say 'the sky is the sea of Brasilia',[3] and it offers a constantly changing spectacle.

The phytogeographic formation of the area is classified as *cerrado* or savanna. It is an arid zone, its ground a mixture of sand and red earth, its vegetation xerophilous[4] – low and stunted, with thick cork bark and few leaves. Hitherto there had been no tradition of transplanting this type of flora into formal gardens.

The rains are torrential, but only in summer. To ameliorate the climate it was necessary to create shade and above all large areas of water. The soil needed protection against drought with creeping ground-cover plants. So the dry, hot climate of Brasilia was modified with artificial lakes, large areas of trees and many gardens. 'The city creates the landscape', wrote Lúcio Costa.[5]

The 'garden-city' developed according to a dynamic equilibrium, in a dialectic of solid and void, seeking a balance between vertical and horizontal planes.

[left] Sunset in Brasilia with a Cerrado tree.

Itamaraty - Ministry of Foreign Affairs

Location Brasilia

Date 1965

Architecture Oscar Niemeyer

Area of external garden 16,000m²

In this dry climate water is crucial. The Itamaraty building stands in the middle of a large rectangular lake which transforms the arches of the façade into harmonious ellipses. Fleeting clouds are reflected in the lake and it is home to many varieties of fish.

The garden is floating: its planters are geometric islands filled with aquatic and damp-soil plants collected in the countryside around Brasilia. Access to the building is over bridges. To the side are local species of palm tree, 'burití' *Mauritia vinifera*, which were successfully transplanted when they were 8 metres tall.

Two more gardens complete the landscape design. One, interior but open to the outside, is a big vertical space under the arches at the back of the building. The vegetation of the humid jungle has been reproduced, with epiphyte plants climbing metal columns rising from a small interior lake. Between the columns are waterfalls at various levels.

The other garden, on a white terrace, is the negative of the ground-level aquatic garden. Its islands are formed of coloured stones and xerophilous plants and an enormous pergola filters the sunlight.

Drawing based on the original plan.

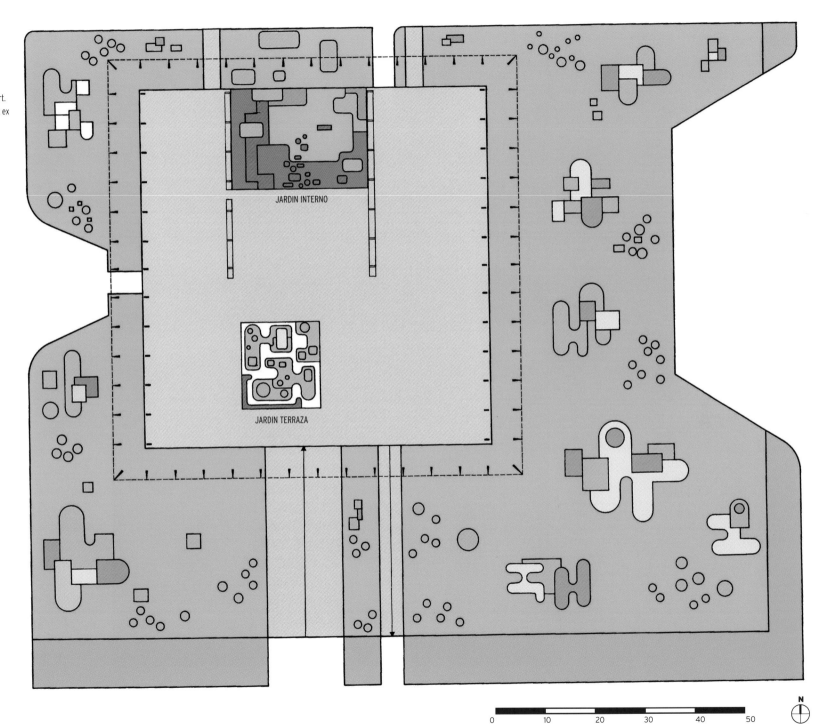

Plant List (partial)

Interior garden
Agave attenuata Salm-Dyck.
Crinum powellii Hort.
Hibiscus rosa-sinensis L. var. cooperi Hort.
Philodendron mellobarretoanum B. Marx ex
   G. H. Barroso
Philodendron selloum C. Koch.
Plumbago capensis Thunb.
Strelitzia reginae Banks.
Zebrina purpusii Brueckner.

Aquatic garden
Cortaderia selloana Aschers et Graebn
Crinum asiaticum L.
Echinodorus macrophyllus Kunth.
Gynerium sagittatum Gilg.
Maranta makoyana Morr.
Nymphaea rudgeana G.F.W. Mey
Reussia rotundifolia Castell.
Sesbanea exasperata H.B.K.
Setcreasea purpurea B.K. Boom.
Spathiphyllum friedschtalli Schott.
Typhonodorum lindleyanum Schott.
Victoria cruziana D'Orbign.

Terrace garden
Carludovica palmata Ruiz et Pav.
Cordilyne terminalis Kunth.
Davalia fijeensis Hook.
Ophiopogon jaburan Lodd.
Ophiopogon japonicus Ker.-Gawl.
Pilea cadierei Gagnep.
Polypodium heracleum Kze.
Xanthosoma lindenii Engl.

JARDIN INTERNO

JARDIN TERRAZA

N

0   10   20   30   40   50

[Left] The terrace with *Clusia fluminensis, Ceiba erianthos* and *Vriesia imperialis*, with sculpture by Maria Martins.

[left] A variety of mineral textures contrast with a compact mass of ferns.

[opposite] The lake that encircles the building, containing islands of *Cyperus prolifer, Allamanda purpurea* and *Canna glauca*.

Ministry of the Army

Location Brasilia

Date 1970

Architecture Oscar Niemeyer,

Area 100,000m²

In the square for the Ministry of the Army Burle Marx composed a dynamic geometrical garden based on a triangular motif, following the shape of the site. It features strongly contrasting colours. The floor surfaces, anticipating large concentrations of people, are laid with Portuguese stone and granite slabs. They are traversed by strictly linear plant beds with brightly coloured foliage.

A lake, essential in this climate, was dug into the centre of the area. Its vast, smooth surface is ruptured by groups of reinforced-concrete sculptures, some acting as supports for aquatic plants. These volumes, inspired by the shapes of crystals, are a symbolic tribute to the mineral riches of Goiás, the state in which Brasilia lies.

Of the many hydrophilic[6] and hygrophilic[7] regional plants proposed, only a small number could be planted. However, large adult specimens of 'burití', the local palm tree which grows by rivers and streams in the savanna, were successfully transplanted, as well as a carpet of ornamental grasses with leaves similar in shape to those of the palms. These silhouettes, when reflected in the water, trace cadenced rhythms that counterbalance the centrifugal impression of the sculptures. Here the water is sky, returning to water when it is ruffled by the wind, blurring the reflections.

Original plan by Burle Marx.

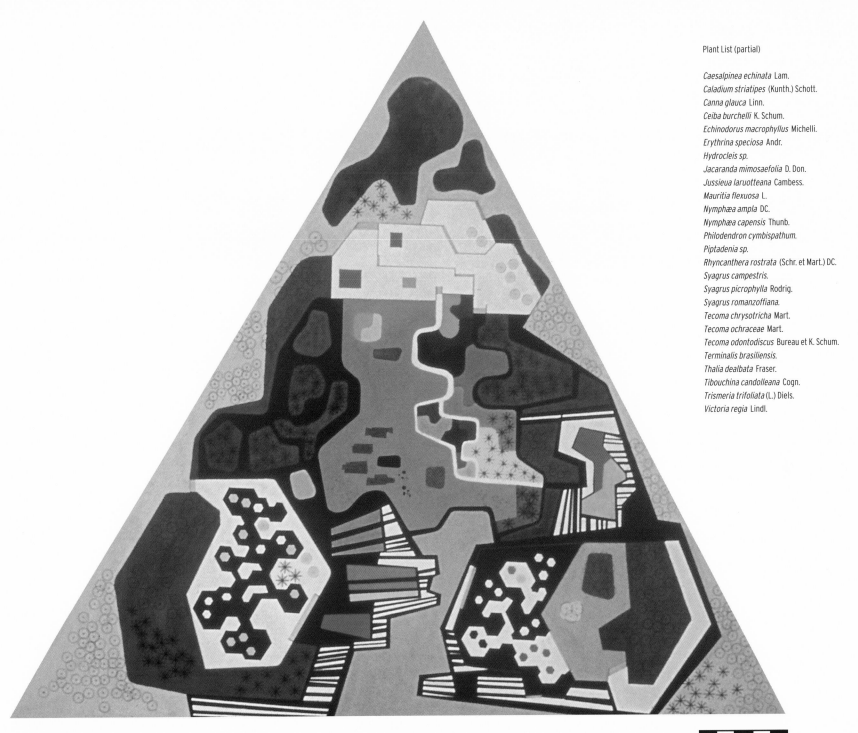

Plant List (partial)

Caesalpinea echinata Lam.
Caladium striatipes (Kunth.) Schott.
Canna glauca Linn.
Ceiba burchelli K. Schum.
Echinodorus macrophyllus Michelli.
Erythrina speciosa Andr.
Hydrocleis sp.
Jacaranda mimosaefolia D. Don.
Jussieua laruotteana Cambess.
Mauritia flexuosa L.
Nymphæa ampla DC.
Nymphæa capensis Thunb.
Philodendron cymbispathum.
Piptadenia sp.
Rhyncanthera rostrata (Schr. et Mart.) DC.
Syagrus campestris.
Syagrus picrophylla Rodrig.
Syagrus romanzoffiana.
Tecoma chrysotricha Mart.
Tecoma ochraceae Mart.
Tecoma odontodiscus Bureau et K. Schum.
Terminalis brasiliensis.
Thalia dealbata Fraser.
Tibouchina candolleana Cogn.
Trismeria trifoliata (L.) Diels.
Victoria regia Lindl.

0   10   20   30   40   50

[left] View over the lake showing *Nymphæa hibrida, Syagrus picrophylla* and, behind, the local palm trees, 'buritís' or *Mauritia flexuosa.*

[left] Concrete sculptures burst from the lake, which contains *Allamanda neerifolia, Clusia sp.,* and *Russelia equisetiformis.*

[opposite] The vast square with geometrical patterns in contrasting colours and linear planters containing *Iresine herbstii, Lantana camara* and *Wedelia trilobata.*

National Fiscal Tribunal

Location Brasilia

Date 1972-73

Architecture Renato Alvarenga

Area 62,000m²

The landscaping scheme for the National Fiscal Tribunal included the transformation of the building's many-levelled terraces into mirrors of water, linked by powerful, noisy waterfalls. These contrast with the light, feathery appearance of surrounding plants. Geometrically shaped islands were built into the pools, containing ground-cover plants of a single colour. A courtyard situated on the upper level was moulded into concave and convex shapes, with areas of earth planted with bushes and epiphytes. The undulating, white stone floor contrasts violently with the black, shiny, perpendicular planes of the surrounding façades.

Drawing based on the original plan.

Plant List (partial)

Acrocomia sclerocarpa Mart.
Caladium striatipes Schott.
Cortaderia selloana Aschers et Graebn
Costus sp. (pink).
Crinum asiaticum L.
Erythrina crista-galli L.
Hedychium coronarium Koen.
Hemerocallis fulva L.
Hydrocleis humboldtiana.
Lantana camara L. (white).
Lantana camara L. (red).
Peltophorum dubium Taub.
Pithecolobium tortum Mart.
Pontederia cordata L.
Syagrus picrophylla Rodrig.
Tecoma caraiba Mart.
Tecoma chrysotricha Mart.
Tibouchina fothergillae Cogn.
Vriesea reginae Beer.
Zoysia matrella Druce.

Upper terrace

0   10   20   30   40   50

N

[left] Water terrace with planters of *Hemerocallis flava, Crinum, Wedelia paludosa, Alcalypha wilkesiana, Lantana camara* and *Allamanda neerifolia.*

[left] The undulating courtyard with *Dicksonia sellowiana, Schizocentron elegans, Zoysia matrella* and *Philodendron mellobarretoanum.*

[opposite] Water falls from the upper terrace over a series of pools surrounded by *Cortaderia selloana.*

National Theatre, Brasilia

Location Brasilia

Date 1976

Architecture Oscar Niemeyer

Area 60,000m²

A climber had embraced a statue of Vertumno, veiling her and covering her with a cloak of leaves in folds that fell so gracefully a sculptor could have used them for a study.

NATHANIEL HAWTHORNE

The garden encircling the National Theatre is planted with drought-resistant vegetation. Inside the theatre, a roof of transparent glass transforms the lobby into a greenhouse. The atmosphere here changes: it is like a stage-set of plants. In the humidity, creepers of diverse textures and colours extend like carpets, climbing and covering cylindrical forms to create mysterious statues, like the drapes that envelop veiled sculptures. Other plants dangle from the mezzanine like the fringes of a curtain. Even when there are no people, the plants in this strange place seem to provide an audience.

[far left] The greenhouse lobby with *Scindapsus aureus, Chlorophitum, Ophiopogum japonicus, Philodendron erubescens* and *Chamaedorea tepijilote*.

[left] Sculpture by Marianne Peretti seen beneath a fringe of plants hanging from the mezzanine.

[opposite] Drawing based on the original plan.

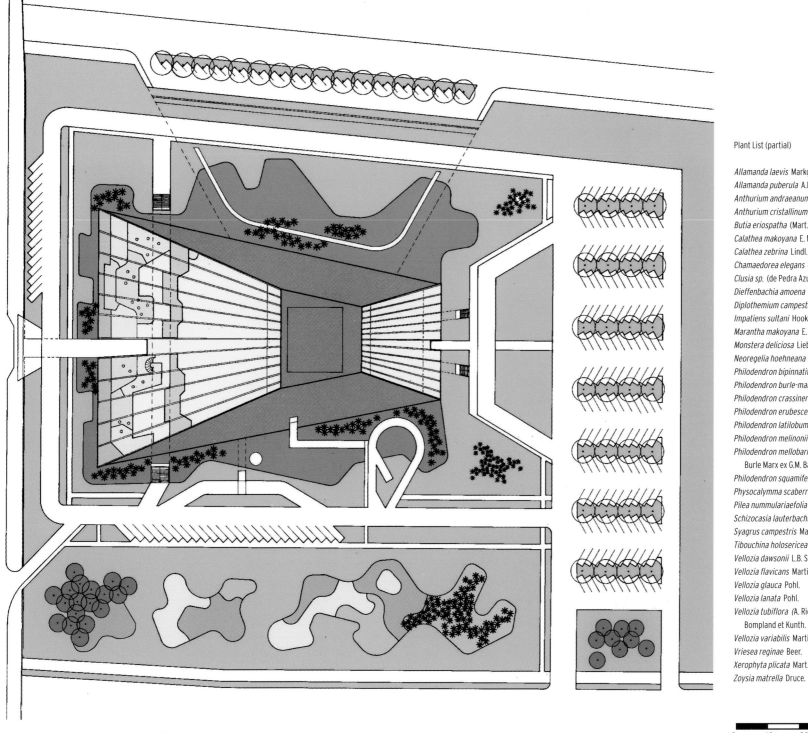

Plant List (partial)

Allamanda laevis Markgraf.
Allamanda puberula A.D.C. in DC.
Anthurium andraeanum Linden.
Anthurium cristallinum Linden et André.
Butia eriospatha (Mart.) Becc.
Calathea makoyana E. Morr.
Calathea zebrina Lindl.
Chamaedorea elegans Mart.
Clusia sp. (de Pedra Azul)
Dieffenbachia amoena Hort. et Gentil.
Diplothemium campestris Mart.
Impatiens sultani Hook.
Marantha makoyana E. Morr.
Monstera deliciosa Liebm.
Neoregelia hoehneana L.B. Smith.
Philodendron bipinnatifidum Schott.
Philodendron burle-marxii G.M. Barroso.
Philodendron crassinervium Lindl.
Philodendron erubescens C. Koch. et Augustin.
Philodendron latilobum Schott.
Philodendron melinonii Brongn.
Philodendron mellobarretoanum
    Burle Marx ex G.M. Barroso.
Philodendron squamiferum Poepp. et Endl.
Physocalymma scaberrimum Pohl.
Pilea nummulariaefolia Wedd.
Schizocasia lauterbachiana Engl.
Syagrus campestris Mart.
Tibouchina holosericea Baill.
Vellozia dawsonii L.B. Smith.
Vellozia flavicans Martius et Schultes.
Vellozia glauca Pohl.
Vellozia lanata Pohl.
Vellozia tubiflora (A. Richard) Humboldt.
    Bompland et Kunth.
Vellozia variabilis Martius et Schultes.
Vriesea reginae Beer.
Xerophyta plicata Mart.
Zoysia matrella Druce.

0   10   20   30   40   50

Plaza República del Perú

Location Buenos Aires, Argentina

Date 1972

Area 7,000m²

Mural 75 x 13m

Buenos Aires: Incalculable Labyrinth

Clothed in cement, shod with metal,
the city yields to me its spiral tango.

LEOPOLDO MARECHAL

'"What the barbarians didn't do, the Barberini did." This phrase, coined in Rome, referred to the destruction of imperial temples by sixteenth-century popes to provide marble and bronze for their resplendent Baroque churches.' Thus begins 'The Barberini in Buenos Aires', an article by the architect Roberto Segre about the partial demolition of the Plaza República del Perú. Segre continues, 'Without wishing to establish a kinship between popes and mayors, the destruction of the only example in Buenos Aires of the creativity of an extraordinary artist is unforgivable.' In fact, this was not the only act of barbarism. Little remains of the original plant selection in the gardens commissioned from Burle Marx's practice by the architect Roberto Aisenson for several apartment blocks in Scalabrini Ortiz and Seguí streets. This work was directed by another of Burle Marx's Argentinian disciples, the landscape designer Dorotea Schultz.

The above-mentioned article was only one of many voices that decried the demolition. The main Brazilian newspapers, *Folha de São Paulo*, *O Estado de São Paulo* and *Jornal do Brasil*, as well as the Argentine Association of Architects in Buenos Aires, lecturers from the departments of Agronomy and Architecture and Urbanism at Buenos Aires University and

Drawing based on the original plan.

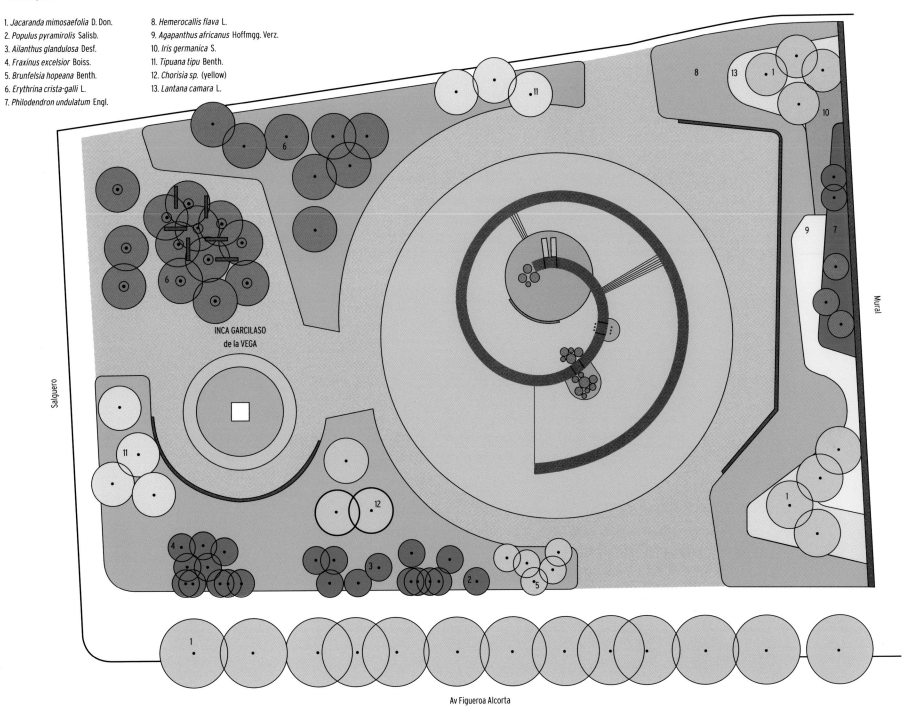

Plant list (partial)

1. *Jacaranda mimosaefolia* D. Don.
2. *Populus pyramirolis* Salisb.
3. *Ailanthus glandulosa* Desf.
4. *Fraxinus excelsior* Boiss.
5. *Brunfelsia hopeana* Benth.
6. *Erythrina crista-galli* L.
7. *Philodendron undulatum* Engl.
8. *Hemerocallis flava* L.
9. *Agapanthus africanus* Hoffmgg. Verz.
10. *Iris germanica* S.
11. *Tipuana tipu* Benth.
12. *Chorisia sp.* (yellow)
13. *Lantana camara* L.

INCA GARCILASO
de la VEGA

Salguero

Mural

Av Figueroa Alcorta

0   5   10   15   20

N

even Burle Marx's practice in Rio de Janeiro, all made their protests heard.

It is no coincidence that this destruction was meted on the only square of many along Avenida Figueroa Alcorta that did not conform to a traditional layout. The design, as well as reflecting Burle Marx's sense of poetry, expressed the relationship between Modernism and the city, which was key to the South American concept of urban design in the twentieth century, of which Burle Marx was a pioneer.

The dimensions of the Plaza República del Perú are modest compared to another of Burle Marx's works, the 70-hectare Parque del Este in Caracas, but it is no less important as a work of art. It is a little gem of ingenuity and creativity, a genuine example of Modernism adapted to Latin America and the spirit of Buenos Aires. It promoted the ideal of South American unity many years before the establishment of the South American common market, Mercosur.

Its rectangular site was previously occupied by a transport company. It was small and inhospitable, boxed into an area of old warehouses and blocks of flats. The volume of surrounding traffic made it very noisy and hazardous.

Given that the enormous Tres de Febrero Park lay nearby, measuring 200 hectares with an abundance of trees, Burle Marx's idea was to create a paved plaza which would be a place for recreational activities for people of all ages. Using architectural and pictorial elements and autochthonous plants, he made an oasis in the middle of a built-up area. Its motifs conjure up Jorge Luis Borges' labyrinth, firing children's imaginations, challenging their spirit of adventure to climb walls and explore volumes.

The site was unusual in the colonial urban planning of Buenos Aires: a rectangle surrounded by streets on three sides with a high party wall on the fourth side. This wall had a geometric outline showing the shape of the roof of the adjacent building, a shed. Burle Marx preserved this sort of *bas-relief* and took it as inspiration for the pattern of a huge mural which covered the whole surface.

In an attempt to balance the Peruvian cultural theme with an area for relaxation and a children's playground, Burle Marx designed a square containing alternating green spaces and dry areas to distinguish different activities. On the most visible and busy corner, Figueroa Alcorta Avenue and Salguero Street, a white marble statue of the Inca Garcilaso was erected, made specially in Rome for this square by the Peruvian sculptor Roca Rey. The opposite corner, the quietest until a shopping centre was built, was conceived as a rest area with coral trees shading benches beneath. A very long, amusingly shaped concrete bench wound its way, snake-like, beside a path in the shade of jacaranda trees.

In the middle, away from the avenue, a cement spiral with a sandpit was built as a protected play area. The idea was to create a space where young children would be sheltered from the heavy traffic. The result was the spiral as symbolic refuge, announcing 'children playing here'.

Burle Marx's design for this 'square with a back' proposed a plastic treatment of vertical and horizontal planes. He used a vibrant palette of colours – red, black and white for the vertical planes and ochre, green and grey for the horizontal. For the flower and plant colours he began with the existing blue-violet of the jacarandas on the pavement alongside and complemented it with the red of coral trees and yellow of day lilies, lantanas and irises. The entirety was arranged like a piece of sculpture. An ascending ramp with various ingenious moulded volumes was an invitation to play. Benches and planters on different levels broke up the horizontal plane, mounting towards the gigantic mural. The square suffered its first amputation when the adjacent building was pulled down, and with it the mural.

This mini-amusement park, its sturdy but exciting shapes reflecting fantasies and dreams of adventure, was a tribute to children in a city of excess – in perpetual metamorphosis, indifferent and hurried. Because Buenos Aires is a city which is continually being destroyed, where the past is wiped out with extraordinary speed.

In this context, the demolition of the Plaza República del Perú seems a normal everyday event, sanctioned by the city's own inhabitants, unaware of the tremendous significance of such an act. Yet while it is legitimate to criticize a work of art, to destroy one is never justified.

The opening near the square of the Latin American Museum of Art by the collector Eduardo Costantini in 2001 may lead the way for the reparation of the past and completion of the unfinished masterpiece. 'I am like the city, constantly making and unmaking myself,' explained the writer Eduardo Mallea.

[left] Bird's-eye view of the Plaza, taken in 1980.

[far left] Slides and sandpit in the central play area.

[left] The construction of the mural on the walled side of the Plaza.

[left] The cement spiral play area with the mural behind.

Chapter Five

Private Gardens

There, all is loveliness and harmony,
Enchantment, pleasure and serenity.

CHARLES BAUDELAIRE

At first sight it is the aesthetic quality
of the private gardens that Roberto Burle
Marx designed which is most impressive.
They transmit an intense sensation of
beauty. Mostly created in wonderful natural
landscapes, they blend so perfectly with
the environment that they seem to
have been there forever.

Detail of Burle Marx's drawing for the Louis Wallerstein Residence
in Teresópolis, 'The Bathers', 1938.

Odette Monteiro Residence[8]

Location Corrêas, Rio de Janeiro

Dates 1948 and 1988

Architecture Wladimir Alves de Souza

Area 50,000m²

Current owner Luiz César Fernandes

One of Burle Marx's most famous gardens was created for his great friend Odette Monteiro. After her death and forty years after the garden was built, the new owner asked Burle Marx to take on the job of restoring it. It is an example of a garden's vulnerability.

The house stands in the middle of a spectacular valley, surrounded by the Serra dos Orgãos, an oft-painted range of sinuous granite mountains. In this region, 800 metres above sea level, the temperature is always ten degrees lower than nearby Rio de Janeiro. The wind can make the light change several times in the course of an hour.

The local flora is predominantly rock plants: *Veloziaceae, Bromeliaceae and Melastomataceae*. A river acts as the boundary of the land. The design was devised using elements already in the landscape, preserving the existing topography, and moulding the terrain only to alter the course of the river to feed an artificial lake in front of the house.

The magic of the whole garden stems from the lake. It mirrors the distinctive profile of the rocks and the continually changing sky, becoming a garden of leaves and clouds. A winding path leads from the house, crossing the lake and continuing up to the highest point of the garden. There it forks, returning to the house on different levels to provide views of the landscape both from the top of the slope and from the bottom.

Vegetation[9] has been planted in clumps by the water, or following the natural slope of the landscape in the groups of painterly, curved beds with massed plants that have made the garden famous. These form monochrome blocks with flowers or leaves in contrasting colours.

Original plan by Burle Marx.

The outlines of the herbaceous borders echo the undulating silhouette of the hills, and the plant selection repeats the tones of the trees flowering on the hillsides. In this way Burle Marx harmonized the garden and the landscape, creating a dialogue between the two.

Near the house, the pink and white of the architecture is repeated in the colours of the plants: azaleas, lilacs, bougainvilleas, petunias, magnolias and a group of extraordinary false silk cotton trees *Pseudobombax ellipticum*, with fuchsia-coloured flowers and leaves that are coppery when they first sprout.

The perspective is deceptive; distant parts of the garden seem close because there are no objects in between to help define the real distance; the boundaries are invisible. The entire vast landscape is captured and incorporated into the design by the reflection of the lake.

[left] Clumps of *Agave weikeii* and *Agave attenuata*.

[opposite] A path crosses the lake before forking at the highest point in the garden; the higher path has borders of *Iresine herbstii* and *Helichrysum petiolatum*.

[left] View of the garden in winter: *Tibouchina granulosa, var. rosea* seen against the lake and, in the foreground, succulent plants *Agave attenuata, Mesembryanthemum roseum* and *Agave americana.*

[left] The garden without boundary, receding towards the silhouette of the Serra dos Orgãos. The colours of the original trees in the surrounding landscape are repeated in the flower beds.

[opposite] The constant motion of the clouds is reflected in the lake.

Olivo Gomes Residence (now Roberto Burle Marx Park)

Location São José dos Campos, São Paulo

Dates 1950 and 1966

Architecture Rino Levi and Associates,

Roberto de Cerqueira César and Roberto de Carvalho Franco

Area 135,000m²

Current owner Municipality of São José dos Campos

The architecture and landscaping of the Olivo Gomes Residence were conceived simultaneously, so the house, murals and gardens all form an integrated whole.

Like the English landscaped garden – which reacted against the formalism of the times, reflecting a desire for a return to nature and a freer use of form – the Olivo Gomes garden has a Romantic air. This is accentuated by its haphazard winding paths, which invite the visitor to wander and dream. Large curved areas, carpeted with ground-cover plants of different colours and textures, further emphasize this impression. Luxuriant, compact masses in a single colour (their impact heightened by their contrasting reflections in the lakes) are juxtaposed to create an intense vibrancy. Important regional trees were planted ('guapuruvú' *Schizolobium parahybum)* as well as aquatic plants in the lakes. The colours and shapes of the plants in the beds are echoed in the tile murals that Burle Marx designed especially for this house.

The project was augmented in 1966 with a games area, swimming pools, fountains and an amphitheatre in a more geometrical style.

Original plan by Burle Marx.

Plant List (partial)

Acrocomia sclerocarpa Mart.
Canna generalis.
Dendrocalamus giganteus Munro.
Erythrina crista-galli L.
Erythrina falcata Benth.
Erythrina speciosa Presl.
Euterpe edulis.
Euterpe edulis Mart.
Euterpe oleraceae.
Helichrysum petiolatum.
Hemerocallis flava L.
Holocalyx glaziovii Taub.
Iresine herbstii.
Jacaranda mimosaefolia D. Don.
Paspalum notatum Fluegge.
Phormium tenax Forst var. atropurpureum Hort.
Piptadenia colubrina.
Roystanea regia O.F. Cook L.C.
Salvia splendens Sellow.
Schizolobium parahybum.
Setcreasea purpurea.
Tabebuia chrysotricha Mart .
Tibouchina fothergillae Cogn.
Tibouchina radula Mgf.
Vriesia imperialis E. Morr.
Vriesia reginae Beer.
Zoysia japonica Steud.

0   50   100

[left] *Thyphonodorum lindleyanum* emerging from the lake beside a colonnade of *Schizolobium parahybum*.

[opposite] A group of native trees *Schizolobium parahybum*.

[left] Detail of *Typhonodorum lindleyanum.*

[left] Patches of colour: amidst the grey of *Helichrysum petiolatum,* a clump of *Canna generalis.*

[opposite] A group of *Canna glauca* surrounded by *Hemerocallis flava* and, behind, palm trees *Euterpe edulis* and *Euterpe oleraceae.*

Celso Colombo Residence

Location   Itanhangá, Rio de Janeiro

Dates   1965, 1981 and 1987

Architecture   Marcello Fragelli

Area   1,650m²

Burle Marx created three separate but communicating gardens at the Celso Residence over a period of twenty-two years, all for the same family. The gardens are relatively small. They share an internal order and harmony that comes from a precise and meticulous mix of plants. The planting scheme differs from that of the larger-scale gardens: plants are not bunched together - each is chosen for its own special features and planted in isolation so that it stands out when observed at close quarters (for example, eye-catching bark or rare flowers).

The repertoire of plants selected by Burle Marx for the first of the three gardens was reiterated in the other two. The most recent of the gardens was planned in collaboration with the architect who designed the house, Marcello Fragelli. The garden penetrates the interior space, which in turn merges with the exterior, blurring the boundaries between the two. Through the interaction of interior and exterior, a homogeneous unit is formed.

Drawing based on the original plan.

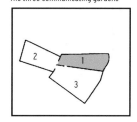

The three communicating gardens

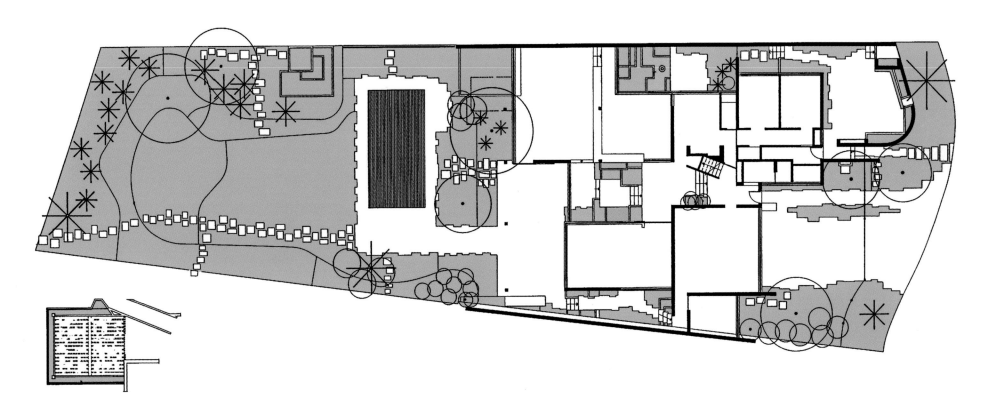

0 1 2 3 4 5

N

Plant List (partial)

Acacia seyal Delile.
Anthurium plowmanii Croat
Barleria cristata L.
Brunfelsia hopeana Benth.
Bulbine sp. (orange).
Calathea kegeliana.
Calathea makoyana.
Calathea sp.
Chamaedorea erumpens H.E. Moore.
Crinum amabile Donn.

Cocos nucifera L.
Costus sp. (white).
Costus sp. (yellow).
Crescentia cujete L.
Encephalartos altensteinii Lehm.
Gardenia jasminoides Ellis.
Hemerocallis flava L.
Licuala grandis H. Wendl.
Liriope muscari L.H. Bailey.
Mussaenda sp. (white).

Mussaenda sp. (red).
Neomarica caerulea Sprague.
Neoregelia sp.
Philodendron bipinnatifidum Schott.
Philodendron latilobum Schott.
Philodendron speciosum Schott.
Philodendron squamiferum Poepp. et Endl.
Philodendron talamancae.
Philodendron wilsonii.
Pilea cadierei Gagnep.

Pinanga kuhlii Blume.
Pithecolobium tortum Mart.
Porphyrocoma pohliana Lindau.
Schefflera actinophylla F. Muell.
Schizocentron elegans Meissn.
Thunbergia grandiflora Roxb.

[far left] The entrance area of the house with stairs from street level.

[left] *Vriesia imperialis* beside a group of *Nolina*.

[far left] Detail of the interior garden with columns of bromeliads, *Scindapsus aureus*, *Xanthosoma lindoni*, *Calathea makoyana* and *Philodendron*.

[left] One of the paths that link the three gardens.

[opposite] The horizontal and vertical circulation zones of the house are covered by a glass roof and filled with a profusion of plants: *Diefenbachia picta*, *Philodendron squamiferum*, *Anthurium plowmanii* and *Peperonia*. Behind, full-height windows open onto the garden.

Mangrove Fazenda

Location   Vista Chinesa, Tijuca Forest, Rio de Janeiro

Date   1974 and 1989

Architecture   Iván Gil de Mello e Souza

Current owner   Nininha Magalhães Lins

The garden of this weekend house was one of the few to be designed *in situ*, without any preliminary plans. It is situated in the heart of the Tijuca Forest.

The basic premise of the design was to accentuate a clearing around the house, which had originally been wrested from the forest. At the borders of the garden, Burle Marx planted transparent, undulating curtains of palm trees and giant bamboos, which interpenetrate the jungle, both integrating and isolating the garden at the same time. Bamboo is also used to conceal the driveways and car park.

The plants on the edges of the composition have been carefully selected, and it could be said that it is there that the real garden lies.

The central area, on a gentle natural slope, is laid with a lawn of strong, tough grass, comfortable underfoot, with no paths. Around this, homogeneous areas of plants are arranged in progressive strata leading up in staggered levels towards the forest. First, the intense green of the grass is halted by undulating clumps of the light leaves of spider plants *Chlorophytum comosum*. From this cloud-like cushion emerge punctilious dark-green *Cycas*. Further up is the negative of this contrast: the white flowers of peace lilies *Spathiphyllum cannaefolium* are framed against their own dark leaves and the red flowers of *Nicolaia elatior* are scattered around.

The spring-water swimming pool clad with boulders.

Mangrove Fazenda

Part of the lawn in the clearing is used as a golf green with bunkers of very fine white sand, one of which holds a dark, aggressive-looking bush, the screw pine *Pandanus utilis.*

Continuing the contrasts, different textures run into each other on the ground: grass extends into the spaces between the granite setts, followed by areas where the setts are laid to a narrow joint. The stones' roughness contrasts with the airiness of the nearby *Liriope muscari.* The original vegetation included purple-coloured glory bushes *Tibouchina* and the plants in the borders respond with pink, violet and white flowers.

A river was diverted to bring spring water closer to the house through a series of locks, one of which forms a swimming pool. A large stone stairway lined with boulders leads into the pool. Its walls are constructed of horizontal stones with grass growing between them. To emphasize the rustic feel of the poolside, groups of irregular stones interrupt any uniformity, with yellow lilies and bromeliads clustered in homogeneous masses to emphasize their formal similarity.

The type of palm tree that was chosen, *Areca catechu*, creates an illusion of light, its bright green leaves standing out against the dark, dense forest. At the other extreme, a lake with huge water lilies either reflects iridescence or shows the darkness of its depths. Through both these effects, Burle Marx uses light to define the garden.

[left] A meandering stream flows towards the house between *Scindapsus aureus, Spathiphyllum candicans* and *Philodendron.*

[opposite] Massed *Liriope muscarii* surround the house.

[left] Clumps of light-leaved *Chlorophytum comosum* contrast with dark-green *Monstera deliciosa*

[left] Plants grouped by formal similarity: *Hemerocallis flava*, *Crinum* and *Vriesia*.

[opposite] The colour of *Neoregelia compacta* illuminates the edges of one of the locks, while *Orquidea cattleya* drapes from the trees.

Vargem Grande Fazenda

Location Areias, São Paulo

Date 1979

Area 9,000m²

Current owner The Gomes family

This garden, built for Clemente F. Gomes, took ten years to complete. It is situated at an altitude of 700 metres in a valley surrounded by mountains 2,000 metres high. The old colonial house - the main building of an abandoned coffee plantation - was restored by Burle Marx, who suggested the tones of the decoration and designed tapestries and stained-glass windows. Very little of the indigenous vegetation had survived, having been sacrificed to coffee cultivation.

According to Burle Marx, it is a 'very structured garden, very severe, and its *leitmotif* is water'. Constant running water is the link between the mountains and the house. The spring that irrigated the land and drove the waterwheels had been preserved as a testimony to the past. And it was the spring and the terraces where the coffee was laid out to dry that inspired the composition.

Lying between the now deforested mountains and the solid, simple architecture of the house, the garden is shaped by the interaction of water, stone and vegetation. Water cascades down a series of twenty water-falls and comes to rest in quiet pools with plants and fish. At the patio beside the house, these small lakes become two swimming pools. Here, a 'Garden of Volumes' is dotted with strange sculpted piles of stone in various textures - rocks, pebbles, boulders - that serve as an infrastructure for bromeliads and orchids. Nature is tamed through the water as it nears the house, and architecture merges into nature through the intermediary of the mineral forms.

Behind the waterfalls a fragrance garden establishes the boundary against the upward slope. Facing downwards from the interior of the house, on clear days you can see a succession of vertical planes - the silhouettes of the mountains. Like an image horizontally reflected, the landscape approaches in waves, with bushes of varying heights interspersed between a colonnade of palm trees.

Original plan by Burle Marx.

A group of tree ferns *Dicksonia sellowiana* (called 'xaxim' in Brazil) that were being stored near the house for use elsewhere spontaneously took root, inspiring the Fern Garden. This small, shady outdoor room is like finely textured underwood, with the bark of the ferns supporting epiphytes.

Amongst the original vegetation can be seen the red coral trees *Erythrina* and the yellow and pink trumpet trees *Tabebuia*. These were also planted in groups around the house, which they illuminate with their spectacular blooms. An important collection of more than twenty-five species of palm tree[10] was also augmented year by year. The swimming pools and the house are connected by a pergola. Red, orange and pink bougainvilleas follow the slope of the valley, cascading from the roof, the trees and the fences.

Like a pivot between memory and imagination, a totem pole of millwheels collected by the fazenda's owner emerges from one of the lakes. This sculpture finds an echo in the giant leaves of the water lilies *Victoria regia*, which are native to the Amazon.

[left] A series of pools with water lilies in the foreground and the swimming pool beyond.

[opposite] A colonnade of imperial palms *Roystonea oleracea* forms the boundary between the garden and the surrounding landscape. Behind is a herbaceous border arranged in layers, with *Crinum plumbago capensis*, *Hemerocallis flava* and coral trees.

[far left] Giant water lilies *Victoria amazonica* and *Cortaderia selloana*.

[left] The swimming pool; its lining is painted green and ocre.

[far left] The totem pole made of old stone millwheels.

[left] The original stone walls of the spring that inspired the composition.

[opposite] The 'Garden of Volumes', shown before completion, with stones and rocks covered with bromeliads, orchids and other epiphytes.

Raul de Souza Martins Residence

Location Petrópolis, Rio de Janeiro

Date 1983

Architecture Raul de Souza Martins

Area 7,000m²

This garden is on a very pronounced slope with a river running through the middle. Access is along a steep incline, flanked on the left by a mountain covered with *Monstera deliciosa*. To the right lies a valley shaded by a forest of ancient trees covered with creepers and lianas that climb trunks, drape from branches and hang between the trees like tattered curtains. At the top of the slope is the house, built on a flat piece of land. Behind it, the mountain continues upwards, as if the architecture were squeezed in between its surroundings.

The owner wanted to create level areas around the house he had inherited from his parents. He built a large cantilevered slab facing west, six metres down the slope, reached by a series of intermediate terraces.

The impression is of a balcony or belvedere, so there is a feeling of vast space even though the valley is not visible through the trees. The terracing of the slopes provides an area for sunbathing, swimming and a bar, with views up into the mountains. Burle Marx maintained the oblique planes of the slope with irregular stepped planters of reinforced concrete, arranged like sculptures to avoid the monotony of a single surface - a treatment that shows the importance of verticality in the composition of a garden.

Next to the house, nestled against the mountain, the brilliance of multi-coloured busy lizzies *Impatiens* moderates the feeling of enclosure. The whole design is completed by a water garden on one side, with aquatic plants and burbling waterfalls, surrounded by a lawn.

Drawing based on the original plan.

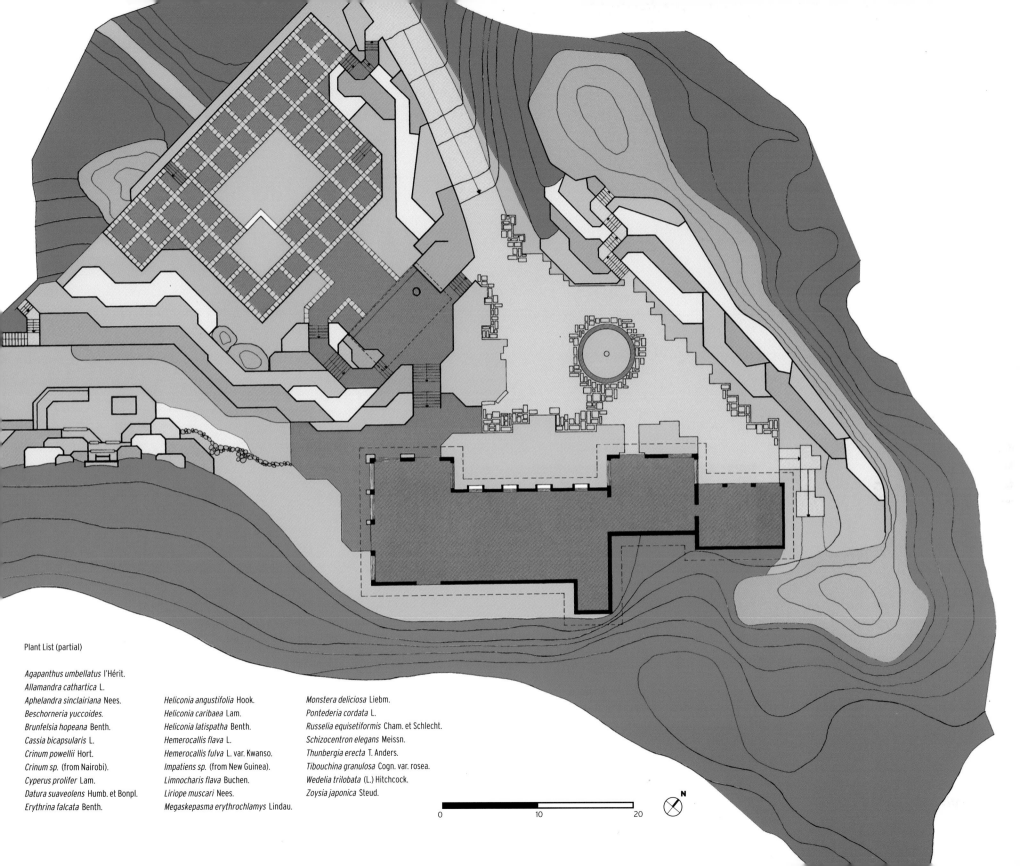

Plant List (partial)

Agapanthus umbellatus l'Hérit.

Allamandra cathartica L.

Aphelandra sinclairiana Nees.

Beschorneria yuccoides.

Brunfelsia hopeana Benth.

Cassia bicapsularis L.

Crinum powellii Hort.

Crinum sp. (from Nairobi).

Cyperus prolifer Lam.

Datura suaveolens Humb. et Bonpl.

Erythrina falcata Benth.

Heliconia angustifolia Hook.

Heliconia caribaea Lam.

Heliconia latispatha Benth.

Hemerocallis flava L.

Hemerocallis fulva L. var. Kwanso.

Impatiens sp. (from New Guinea).

Limnocharis flava Buchen.

Liriope muscari Nees.

Megaskepasma erythrochlamys Lindau.

Monstera deliciosa Liebm.

Pontederia cordata L.

Russelia equisetiformis Cham. et Schlecht.

Schizocentron elegans Meissn.

Thunbergia erecta T. Anders.

Tibouchina granulosa Cogn. var. rosea.

Wedelia trilobata (L.) Hitchcock.

Zoysia japonica Steud.

0   10   20

N

On one of the terraces is a plant sculpture, a metal column with containers painted in primary colours holding epiphytes. This design was originally conceived for an exhibition at the Hayward Gallery in London called 'Art in Latin America'. On a lower terrace, with a surface of interwoven red ceramic and beige marble, are two swimming pools arranged in echelon. Because of the pools' white lining, the water reflects the sky and turns a bright blue. The accompanying facilities - toilets, dining and lounging areas and a bar - are built into the bank. The whole is set off against a vertical plane of tiles designed by Burle Marx, which picks up the pattern of the floors, but predominantly in blue, repeating the colour of the water.

The colour scheme of the leaves and flowers continues these shades, complementing them with greys and yellows. The edge of the balcony is lined with a hedge of a very fine soft-leafed *Russelia*, with small red flowers which complete the trilogy of primary colours. Along the two shorter sides of the terrace, borders stepping up the slopes contain groups of plants of similar textures, colours and shapes, planted in isolation rather than bunched together in homogeneous masses. Large in scale, they are voluminous, filling the space, moving with the wind.

[left] By the house, a soft green carpet of grass surrounds an aquatic garden with *Pontederia cordata*. Planters containing *Heliconia* and *Agapanthus umbellatus* are stepped up the slope.

[far left] The terrace beside the house is bordered with *Liriope muscari.* *Philodendron bipinnatifidum* and *Monstera deliciosa* climb the hillside.

[left] The swimming pools. Concrete planters rising in stages up the slope surround the terrace with vegetation. To the right is the balcony looking over the valley.

[far left] A view of the successive terraces built into the hillside with a plant sculpture visible to the right.

[left] The aquatic garden, with *Cyperus prolifer* and *Pontederia cordata.* Palm trees *Aiphanes caryotaefolia* against the mountainside, with *Monstera deliciosa,* *Aphelandra sinclairiana* and *Impatiens* covering the slope.

Chapter Six

The Garden of Wonders

A garden of living, palpitating beauty and such wondrous refinement that it made you dream of a race of diligent fairies. EDGAR ALLAN POE

Detail of Burle Marx's drawing
for the Louis Wallerstein Residence in
Teresópolis, 'Woman in a Hammock', 1938.

Santo Antônio da Bica (now Roberto Burle Marx Foundation)

Location   Guaratiba, Rio de Janeiro

Date   Begun 1949

Area   365,000m²

Burle Marx's own garden was in a state of perpetual motion. Every morning he would go round reshaping, reinventing it. This made it completely different from his clients' gardens, in which evolution – apart from the growth of the plants themselves – was neither envisaged nor desired. Other people's gardens were created to titillate the senses – orderly gardens, which calmed the power of rampant nature and the chaos of the city. Nature was tamed in his gardens but it was given the utmost respect. This was his way of shouting a warning, pleading for nature's conservation – if one loves a tree one would never destroy it.

Santo Antônio da Bica, situated 60 kilometres from the centre of Rio, is reached along the lower part of a northwesterly slope. Beside the access road, Burle Marx laid out 6,000 square metres of nursery gardens – greenhouses, seed beds and propagators – to house the plants which formed part of his collection and to serve as wombs for cultivating the various species. Up the steep slope, he paved a road leading to the house and a seventeenth-century chapel dedicated to Saint Anthony, who gave the place its name. He restored the chapel and opened it to the local people, who go to mass on Sundays and even hold weddings there.

Water spurts from granite stones surmounted by epiphytes, cascading down into a water garden.

The old house looks out over a valley, and on the horizon, beyond the mangrove swamps, is the sea. The building was continually being transformed by the addition of rooms and workshops. Burle Marx had a verandah built – an area of shade, a frontier zone between the garden and the house – over which stand guard four figureheads from boats on the São Francisco River in the north of Brazil. It was on this verandah – continually alive with the sound of wind mobiles – that he arranged his wonderful orchids, replacing them periodically as they came into bloom in the orchidarium.

Roberto liked to recount how he had been very taken with an old wooden door he saw at an auction. He had bought it but then did not know where to put it because it was enormous. So he built a room taller than the house itself where he could finally hang the door. The genesis of his garden was similar. He created spaces to receive certain plants, not the other way round.

The ceiling of the room with the strange door is covered with frescos that Burle Marx painted himself. On the walls hang his paintings from the 1930s and 1940s. A collection of handicrafts from the Jequitinhonha Valley and sculptures of multi-coloured wood by Maurino de Araújo provide a feast for the eyes. Another addition was a new studio built from a seventeenth-century Portuguese granite façade that he rescued from a demolition site in colonial Rio, but he died before he was able to use the studio.

Entering the house you came upon the first of many gardens: ephemeral plant sculptures he created for every occasion. Also there are collections of sacred images, paintings from Cuzco, pre-Columbian pottery, local Brazilian ceramics, pieces of European crystal and others designed by Burle Marx.

The transition from house to landscape is achieved through terraces which interrupt the natural slope of the land. They are perpendicularly structured gardens, edged with granite from old demolished houses, which divide the open spaces. The 'natural landscape' is wild. In contact with the house, the 'constructed landscape' is disciplined.

On a plain lawn, the intricate silhouettes of palms[11] and trees, *Neodypsis decaryi* and *Plumeria sp.* among others, stand out like sculptures. Against the orange-red background of a flame tree *Delonix regia*, blocks of granite are stacked to form a wall of advancing and receding planes, which supports copper-hued rock plants. Water spurts from these stones, cascading down into a water garden.

Behind the house is the area where Burle Marx grouped plants according to their ecological characteristics within small ecosystems. His rock gardens were based on textures, with each plant providing a focal point. Of particular interest among them is a rock garden of xerophilous plants. Large river-polished stones and small boulders create an interplay of contrasts in the composition.

To the south, seeking the cool, Burle Marx had a 'green room' built with a pergola and pools on different levels. Light reflected from clusters of turquoise flowers and the dark green leaves of the climber *Strongylodon macrobotrys* – a plant native to the Philippines – produces an almost magical effect.

The site was originally Atlantic rainforest, cleared to make way for a banana plantation and as you move away from the house the landscape deliberately returns to the wild. The natural slope of the site has been preserved and Burle Marx used huge existing strangely shaped granite rocks and numerous rain-swelled streams to create small lakes feeding into concrete-lined pools, sometimes opening up spaces, sometimes making enclosed environments. He planted, according to the different microclimates (shady, damp or sunny), dense and rich vegetation made up of both foreign and native plants in seeming disarray.

On a daily basis he added or discarded plants, choosing from those which, having come from far afield, were awaiting their turn in the nursery. These plants so resembled strange animals that we can imagine them escaping back into the jungle now that Burle Marx is no longer there.

[above] *Agave attenuata* in bloom in the rock garden.

[far left] The verandah, guarded by prow figures from boats on the São Francisco River, with an ephemeral garden of orchids.

[left] Cycads and bromeliads and the pink bracts from the creeper *Congea tomentosa*.

[far left] The seventeenth-century Portuguese granite façade rescued from a demolition site in colonial Rio and later converted into Burle Marx's studio.

[left] *Marantacea* and *Syagrus*.

[opposite] One of the lakes surrounded by rocks, with groups of bromeliads and *Montrichardia*.

Epilogue

Roberto Burle Marx was born and lived in a huge country, a place where the tropics fire the climate into eternal summer, a continuum where the four seasons do not exist. He was a young man in the period marked by World War II, which left Europe in ruins while the Americas were bathed in the hopeful light of the Promised Land, the world of the future.

This South American 'paradise', as it is perceived from Europe, is, however, plagued by contradictions, contrasts and paradoxes. It is not homogeneous; there are differences and nuances. The luxuriant vegetation and exuberance of Brazil is a far cry from the empty, melancholic vastness of the Argentine pampas.

So tropical Brazil was for me a spectacular and unexpected discovery. I arrived there from Paris, where I was living in exile, and although I was a foreigner, I somehow felt a sense of identification. Brazil was for me a substitute homeland. I felt I had come back to my roots without going to Argentina. Separated from my family, I felt that Burle Marx was an adopted father to me.

While national differences exist, there is also a secret code in Latin America that unites us.

For Brazilians, like Argentines, necessity is the mother of invention, invention is survival. If we don't act we go under. We act because there is no time to think, and because we aren't taught to think.

Burle Marx was extremely privileged to have access to two different and, in those days, very distant worlds: Europe in the 1930s with all its refinement and culture, cauldron of artistic experiment; and South America, where everything was waiting to be done and discovered. He was one of a small group of intellectuals and artists who worked to reshape a country. They did it with spontaneity, intuition and imagination (sometimes to the detriment of critical restraint), taking avant-garde trends from Europe and transforming them irreverently, freely and courageously.

Roberto used to say he had been lucky enough to receive much from life, and that it was his duty to give something back. In *Burle Marx – The Lyrical Landscape,* I wanted to share with the reader the warmth and intensity of the universe he revealed to me and the immense joy of life he radiated. I hope I have succeeded.

Endnotes to Part Two

1. This area is generally known as 'Aterro' in Rio de Janeiro. 'Aterro' means 'infill' in Portuguese.
2. Lúcio Costa, from his first-prize-winning submission for a pilot design for Brasilia, 1957, republished in Costa et al, *Brasilia* (Rio de Janeiro, Edition Alumbramento, 1986).
3. Lúcio Costa, *Registro de una Vivencia* (São Paulo, Ed. Empresa das Artes, 1995).
4. Adapted to a dry climate.
5. Lúcio Costa, op. cit.
6. Living in water.
7. Living in humid soil.
8. Many of the private gardens are identified by the name of the person who originally commissioned them.
9. List of plants at Odette Montero:
   Acalypha wilkesiana, Muell. Arg. var. Musaica Hort.
   Allamanda nobilis Schott.
   Anthurium coriaceum Schott.
   Anthurium sp.
   Arecastrum romanzoffianum (Cham.) Becc.
   Attalea dubia (Mart.) Burret.
   Barbacenia coccinea Mart.
   Barbacenia sp.
   Brassavola perrini Lindl.
   Calathea cylindrica K. Schum.
   Canna indica L. (orange).
   Canna indica L. (red).
   Canna indica L. (yellow).
   Cassia bicapsularis L.
   Cephalocereus fluminensis Britt et Rose.
   Chaetostoma burle-marxii Mello Barreto.
   Chorisia crispiflora H.B.K.
   Clusia fluminensis Tr. et Planch.
   Clusia grandiflora Splitg.
   Cordyline terminalis Kunth.
   Coreopsis grandiflora Nutt.
   Cortaderia selloana Arschers et Groebn.
   Crinum sp. (red).
   Cyperus giganteus Vahl.
   Cyrtopodium andersonii R.-BR.
   Echinodorus macrophyllus Kunth.
   Epidendron wedellii Lindl.
   Eryngium sp.
   Euphorbia fulgens Karw.
   Euphorbia splendens Boj.
   Euterpe edulis Mart.
   Fetos arborescentes.
   Galactia Walleriana Mello Barreto.
   Gymnopteris tomentosa (Lam.) Und.
   Gynerium sagittatum (Aubl.) Beauv.
   Hedychium coccineum Buch.-Ham.
   Heliconia psittacorum L.F.
   Hemerocallis aurantiaca Baker.
   Hemerocallis citrina Baroni.
   Hemerocallis flava L.
   Hemerocallis fulva L.
   Hemerocallis fulva L. var. Kwanso Hort.
   Hippeastrum acuminatum Ker.
   Hippeastrum organensis Hook.
   Hippeastrum procerum Lem.
   Hypoestes sanguinolenta Hook.
   Iresine herbstii Hook.
   Iris germanica L. (blue and white).
   Iris sp. (yellow).
   Jussiaea sp.
   Kniphofia uvaria Hook. (orange).
   Kniphofia uvaria Hook. (yellow).
   Laelia cinnabarina Batem.
   Lantana sp.
   Lavoisiera imbricata (Thunb.) DC.
   Lobelia exaltata Pohl.
   Lobelia organensis Gardn.
   Mandevilla lucida Woods.
   Metternichia principis Mik.
   Moraea bicolor Steud.
   Moraea iridioides L.
   Musa coccinea Andr.
   Myrianthera pulchra Kuhlm.
   Neomarica coerulea Ker.
   Opuntia brasiliensis Haw.
   Paliavana selloana (Hnst.) Fritsch.
   Passiflora violacea Vell.
   Peperomia incana A. Dietr.
   Philodendron undulatum Engl.
   Pitcairnia corcovadensis Wawra.
   Poinsettia pulcherrima Graham.
   Pontederia cordata L.
   Pteris pedata L.
   Rhipsalis mesembryanthemoides Haworth.
   Rhynchanthera rostrata (Schr. et Mart.) DC.
   Rosa (Crimson Glory).
   Rosa (Polyantha).
   Rosa (Sempervirens).
   Salvia splendens Sellow.
   Scleria sp.
   Selaginella convoluta (Arn.) Spring.
   Sinningia speciosa (Lodd.) Benth. et Hook.
   Spartium junceum L.
   Stillingia dichotoma Muell. Arg.
   Strelitzia reginae Banks.
   Tagetes patula L. (orange).
   Tagetes sp. (lemon).
   Tibouchina arborea (Gardn.) Cogn.
   Tibouchina candolleana (Mart.) Cogn.
   Tibouchina canescens (D. Don.) Cogn.
   Tibouchina fothergillae (Schr. et Mart.) Cogn.
   Tibouchina grandiflora Cogn.
   Tibouchina holosericea Baill.
   Tibouchina mutabilis (Vell.) Cogn.
   Tibouchina organensis Cogn.
   Tibouchina sellowiana (Cham.) Cogn.
   Tibouchina semidecandra (Schr. et Mart.) Cogn.
   Tritonia crocata Ker.-Gawl (yellow).
   Tritonia crocosmaeflora Lem.
   Vellozia candida Mik.
   Vellozia plicata Mart.
   Vellozia sp.
   Verbena hybrida Hort. (red).
   Vriesia sp.
   Wedelia paludosa DC. var. vialis DC.
   Wunderlichia sp.
10. List of palm trees at the Vargem Grande Fazenda:
    Acrocomia glaucophylla (São Paulo).
    Aiphanes caryotaefolia.
    Archonthophoenix cunninghamiana.
    Areca catechu.
    Areca vestiaria.
    Arecastrum romanzoffianum 'pindó'.
    Bactris escragnollei sp. 'tucum'.
    Butia sp. 'yatay'.
    Caryota urens. 'fishtail'.
    Chrysalidocarpus lucubensis.
    Chrysalidocarpus lutescens 'butterfly'.
    Cocos nucifera 'bitter heart of palm'.
    Euterpe edulis 'heart of palm'.
    Licuala grandis.
    Licuala spinosa.
    Mascarena verschaffeltii 'bottle'.
    Neodypsis decaryi (Madagascar).
    Pinanga kuhlii (Asia).
    Ptychosperma elegans 'solitaire'.
    Raphia excelsa.
    Raphia vinifera.
    Roystonea oleracea 'imperial palm' (Trinidad).
    Sabal sp.
    Veitchia joanis.
11. List of palm trees at Santo Antônio da Bica:
    Allagoptera arenaria.
    Corypha umbraculifera.
    Cyrtostachys renda 'blood-red palm'.
    Dictyosperma album.
    Euterpe acuminata 'heart of palm'.
    Leopoldinia piassava 'hairy'.
    Livistona chinensis 'Chinese palm'.
    Phoenix canariensis 'phoenix'.
    Phoenix dactylifera 'date palm'.

Chronology of Principal Works

1932

Schwartz Residence

Rio de Janeiro, RJ

Architects: Gregori Warchavchik

and Lúcio Costa

1934-37 Recife, PE

(as Director of Parks and Gardens)

Praça do Derby
Casa Forte Gardens
Pernambuco State Government House
Gardens, Princess's Palace
Parque Dos Hermanos
Praça Arthur Oscar
Praça Euclides da Cunha
Praça República

1938

Ministry of Education and Health

Rio de Janeiro, RJ

Architects: Lúcio Costa, Affonso Reidy, Oscar Niemeyer,

Jorge Machado Moreira, Carlos Leão, Ernani Vasconcellos,

Luis Nunes and Emilio Baumgart.

Architectural consultant: Le Corbusier.

Praça Senador Salgado Filho,
Santos Dumont Airport

Rio de Janeiro, RJ

Architects: Marcelo, Milton

and Mauricio Roberto

Brazilian Press Association

Rio de Janeiro, RJ

Architects: Marcelo and

Milton Roberto

J. Louis Wallerstein
Residence

Teresópolis, RJ

Raymundo de Castro Maia
Residence

Rio de Janeiro

Roberto Marinho
Residence

Rio de Janeiro, RJ

Architect: César Melo Cunha

1939

Brazilian Insurance
Institute Building

Rio de Janeiro, RJ

Architects: Marcelo and Milton Roberto

1940

Parque Solon de Lucena

João Pessoa, PE

1942

Pampulha Complex
Gardens for the casino, yacht club,
ballroom, island restaurant and
Church of São Francisco

Belo Horizonte, MG

Architect: Oscar Niemeyer

Praça de Cataguazes

Cataguazes, MG

Architect: Oscar Niemeyer

João Cavalcanti Residence

Rio de Janeiro, RJ

1943

Araxá Thermal Park

Araxá, MG

In collaboration with the botanist

Henrique Lahmeyer de Mello Barreto

Juscelino Kubitschek
de Oliveira Residence

Belo Horizonte, MG

Architect: Oscar Niemeyer

1946

Zoological botany section,
Zoological Garden

Rio de Janeiro, RJ

In collaboration with the botanist

Henrique Lahmeyer de Mello Barreto

1947

**Gardens for three buildings
in the Parque Guinle**

Rio de Janeiro

Architects: Lúcio Costa and Marcelo,
Milton and Mauricio Roberto

**Jean Marie Diestl
Residence**

Rio de Janeiro, RJ

1948

Samambaia Fazenda

Petrópolis, RJ

Arnaldo Aizim Residence

Rio de Janeiro, RJ

Architect: Paulo Santos

Diego Cisneros Residence

Caracas, Venezuela

Ernesto Waller Residence

Teresópolis, RJ

Odette Monteiro Residence

Corrêas, RJ

Architect: Wladimir Alves de Souza

Burton Tremaine Residence

Santa Barbara, California

Architect: Oscar Niemeyer

1949

Santo Antônio da Bica

Guaratiba, RJ

Mario Martins Residence

Rio de Janeiro, RJ

1950

Vasco de Gama Yacht Club

Rio de Janeiro, RJ

Hotel Amazonas

Manaus, AM

Architect: Paulo Antunes Ribeiro

Hotel da Bahía

Salvador, BA

Architect: Paulo Antunes Ribeiro
and Diógenes Rebouças

Olivo Gomes Residence

São José dos Campos, SP

Architects: Rino Levi and Associates,
Roberto de Cerqueira César and
Roberto de Carvalho Franco

José Carvalho Residence

Petrópolis, RJ

Architect: Henrique Mindlin

**José Piquet Carneiro
Residence**

Rio de Janeiro, RJ

**Ormeo Junqueira
Botelho Residence**

Leopoldina, MG

**Orozimbo Roxo
Loureiro Residence**

São Paulo, SP

1951

**Atrium of the Church of Our Lady
of Conceição da Jaqueira**

Recife, PE

Pedregulho Residential Complex

Rio de Janeiro, RJ

Architect: Affonso Reidy

**Marechal Hermes
Popular Theatre**

Rio de Janeiro, RJ

Architect: Affonso Reidy

Roche Laboratories

Rio de Janeiro, RJ

Air Force Ministry

Galeão Airport, Rio de Janeiro, RJ

**Benjamin David Sion
Residence**

Rio de Janeiro, RJ

**Cassiano Ribeiro
Coutinho Residence**

João Pessoa, PE

Architect: Acácio Gil Borsoi

**Walter Moreira Salles
Residence**

Rio de Janeiro, RJ

Architect: Olavo Redig de Campos

1952

**University of Bahía
Rector's Residence**

Salvador, BA

Praça Independencia

João Pessoa, PE

Praça Terreiro de Jesús

Salvador, BA

Carlos Somlo Residence

Teresópolis, RJ

**Icaro de Castro Mello
Residence**

São Paulo, SP

Architect: Icaro de Castro Mello

Olavo Fontoura Residence

Rio de Janeiro, RJ

1953

Pampulha Airport

Belo Horizonte, MG

**University of Brazil -
University City**

Rio de Janeiro, RJ

Architect: Jorge Machado Moreira

Ceppas Building

Rio de Janeiro, RJ

Architect: Jorge Machado Moreira

Childcare Institute

Rio de Janeiro, RJ

Architect: Jorge Machado Moreira

Galeão Airport

Rio de Janeiro, RJ

US Embassy

Rio de Janeiro, RJ

Parque Ibirapuera

São Paulo, SP

Architect: Oscar Niemeyer

**Alfredo Baumann
Residence**

Teresópolis, RJ

Architect: Wit Olaf Prochnik

**Oscar Niemeyer
Residence**

Rio de Janeiro, RJ

Architect: Oscar Niemeyer

1954

Museum of Modern Art

Rio de Janeiro, RJ

Architect: Affonso Reidy

Largo do Machado

Rio de Janeiro, RJ

Praça Três de Maio
(renovation)

Salvador, BA

**Edmundo Cavanellas
Residence**

Rio de Janeiro, RJ

Architect: Oscar Niemeyer

**Ernesto Waller
Residence**

Rio de Janeiro, RJ

Architect: Paulo Antunes Ribeiro

1955

South American Hospital

Rio de Janeiro, RJ

Architects: Oscar Niemeyer
and Hélio Uchoa

Labor Temple

Los Angeles, California

Architect: Richard Neutra

**Alberto Kronsfoth
Residence**

Teresópolis, RJ

Architect: Julio Zena

Current owner: Ralph Camargo

**Ambassador Sergio Correia
da Costa Residence**

Rio de Janeiro, RJ

Architect: Jorge Machado Moreira

1956

Francisco Pignatari Residence

São Paulo, SP

Architect: Oscar Niemeyer

José T. Nabuco Residence

Rio de Janeiro, RJ

1956-64, Caracas, Venezuela

(Caracas office of Burle Marx Cía Ltda)

**Parque del Este
Parque del Oeste
Inocente Palacios Residence**

1957

Guararapes Airport

Recife, PE

**Gardens of the Monument to
the Fallen of World War II,
Parque do Flamengo**

Rio de Janeiro, RJ

Architect: Marcos Konder Neto

**Carmen B. de Mello Carneiro
da Cunha Residence**

Rio de Janeiro, RJ

Cesário Levy Carneiro Residence

Rio de Janeiro, RJ

Schulthess Residence

Havana, Cuba

Architect: Richard Neutra

1958

**Brazilian Pavilion at the
Brussels International Fair**

Brussels, Belgium

Architect: Sergio Bernardez

Olivetti Factory, playground

Buenos Aires, Argentina

1959

Richard Neutra Residence

Los Angeles, California, USA

Architect: Richard Neutra

1960

**Jorge Machado Moreira
Residence**

Rio de Janeiro, RJ

Architect: Jorge Machado Moreira

1961

Monumental axis

Brasilia, DF

Architects: Oscar Niemeyer
and Lúcio Costa

Parque do Flamengo

Rio de Janeiro, RJ

Working group for the urbanization of the Aterro:
Affonso Reidy, Jorge Machado Moreira, Carlos Werneck
de Carvalho, Helio Mamede, Berta Leitchic,
Luiz Emyglio de Mello Filho, Roberto Burle Marx

1962

Parque de las Americas

Santiago, Chile

1963

**South American
Bank of Brazil**

São Paulo, SP

Architects: Rino Levi and Associates,
Roberto de Cerqueira César and
Roberto de Carvalho Franco

**Terraces for UNESCO
Headquarters**

Paris, France

Architects: Marcel Breuer, Pier Luigi Nervi
and Bernard-Louis Zehrfuss

Garden of Nations

Vienna, Austria

Architect: Karl Mang

1965

**Itamaraty –
Ministry of Foreign Affairs**

Brasilia, DF

Architect: Oscar Niemeyer

Almeida Braga Residence

Rio de Janeiro, RJ

Gomes Brothers Residence

Ubatuba, SP

Architects: Rino Levi and Associates

Otto Dunhoffer Residence

Rio de Janeiro, RJ

Architects: Milton Federman and Paulo Tarso Santos

Regina Feigl Residence

Rio de Janeiro, RJ

Celso Colombo Residence

Itanhangá, RJ

Architect: Marcello Fragelli

1966

Ponte Alta Fazenda

Barra do Piraí, RJ

Souza Aguiar Hospital

Rio de Janeiro, RJ

Architect: Ary García Roza

Manchete Building

Rio de Janeiro, RJ

Architect: Oscar Niemeyer

Civic Centre

Curitiba, PR

Architect: Olavo Rediz de Campos, David Azambuja

Cândido Guinle de Paula Machado

Rio de Janeiro, RJ

Architect: Jorge Hüe

Lygia Andrade Residence

Rio de Janeiro, RJ

Nathan Breitman Residence

Rio de Janeiro, RJ

Odette Padilha Gonçalves Residence

Rio de Janeiro, RJ

1967

Sayonara Building

Rio de Janeiro, RJ

**Federal Resources
Tribunal Building**

Brasilia, DF

Architect: Hugo Montenegro

US Embassy

Brasilia, DF

Formiplac

Rio de Janeiro, RJ

Architects: Rino Levi and Associates,
Roberto de Cerqueira César and
Roberto de Carvalho Franco

Santo André Civic Centre

Santo André, SP

Architects: Rino Levi and Associates

Brazilian Jockey Club

Rio de Janeiro, RJ

Architect: Lúcio Costa

1968

Araucaria Condominiums

São Paulo, SP

Architects: Rino Levi and Associates,
Roberto de Cerqueira César and
Roberto de Carvalho Franco

Gravatá Condominiums

São Paulo, SP

Architects: Rino Levi and Associates,
Roberto de Cerqueira César and
Roberto de Carvalho Franco

Campo das Gardênias Building

Rio de Janeiro, RJ

Architect: Jorge Machado Moreira

Parque Anhembi

São Paulo, SP

Architects: Jorge Wilheim
and Miguel Juliano e Silva

West German Embassy

Brasilia, DF

Architect: Hans Scharoun

**Palace of Lions,
Government House**

São Luis, MA

Praça São Judas Tadeu

Santo André, SP

**Sanctuary Bom Jesus
do Matosinhos**

Congonhas do Campo, MG

Brazilian Embassy

Washington DC, USA

Architect: Olavo Rediz de Campos

Benedito Días Macedo Residence

Fortaleza, CE

Architect: Acácio Gil Borsói

Clemente Gomes Residence

São Paulo, SP

Architects: Rino Levi and Associates,
Roberto de Cerqueira César and
Roberto de Carvalho Franco

Terezinha Ferrari Residence

Rio de Janeiro, RJ

**Bank of Brazil, Ciudad de
San Sebastián Building**

Rio de Janeiro, RJ

Architect: Marcello Graça Couto Campello

Metropolitan Cathedral

Rio de Janeiro, RJ

Architect: Luiz Fabricio Menescal

1969

**Pernambuco Development Bank
Headquarters**

Recife, PE

Architect: Acácio Gil Borsói

Bloch Building

Rio de Janeiro, RJ

Architect: Oscar Niemeyer

Petrobras Building

Rio de Janeiro, RJ

Architects: José María Gandolfi, Luiz Forte Neto,
Roberto Gandolfi, Vicente Ferreira de Castro,
José Sanchotene and Abrão Anizassad

**Confederation of Industry Building
(SESI/FIESP/CIESP)**

São Paulo, SP

Architects: Roberto de Cerqueira César
and Roberto de Carvalho Franco

1970

Copacabana Promenade

Rio de Janeiro, RJ

**Morada do Sol
Residential Complex**

Rio de Janeiro, RJ

Morwan Building

Rio de Janeiro, RJ

Architect: Jorge Machado Moreira

Syrian Sports Club

São Paulo, SP

Architects: Pedro Paulo de Mello Saraiva,
Miguel Juliano and Silva and Sami Bussab

Hilton Hotel

São Paulo, SP

Ministry of the Army

Brasilia, DF

Architect: Oscar Niemeyer

Parque Central

Caracas, Venezuela

Architects: Siso, Shaw and Associates

1971

Sheraton Hotel

Rio de Janeiro, RJ

Architect: Henrique Mindlin

Parque Estatal de Torres

Porto Alegre, RS

Belgian Embassy

Brasilia, DF

Architect: Paulo Antunes Ribeiro

Iranian Embassy

Brasilia, DF

1972

Bahía Othon Palace Hotel

Salvador, BA

Architects: Paulo Casé
and Luiz Acioli Associates

**Northeast Administrative
and Development Office**

Recife, PE

Usiminas Headquarters

Belo Horizonte, MG

Architects: Rafael and Alvaro Hardy

**Social and Commercial
Services Building**

Rio de Janeiro, RJ

Architects: Sergio Jamel, Marco Antonio Coelho da Silva,
Mario de Lourdes Davies de Freitas and
Angela Tamega Menezes

Intercontinental Hotel

Rio de Janeiro, RJ

Architect: Henrique Mindlin

Industria Merck

Rio de Janeiro, RJ

**Karnack State
Government House**

Teresina, PI

Plaza República del Perú

Buenos Aires, Argentina

Plaza Brasilia

Quito, Ecuador

**Santa Tereza
Tram Terminal**

Rio de Janeiro, RJ

Architects: Flavio Marinho do Rego
and Paulo Conde

Rio Othon Palace Hotel

Rio de Janeiro, RJ

Architects: Pontual Associates
Architects and Planners

National Fiscal Tribunal

Brasilia, DF

Architect: Renato Alvarenga

Carl Fischer Residence

Rio de Janeiro, RJ

**Wenceslau Verde
Martinez Residence**

Rio de Janeiro, RJ

1973

Fortaleza Municipality Building

Fortaleza, CE

United Nations Avenue Complex

São Paulo, SP

Architects: Botti and Rubin Associates

Curitiba Bus Station

Curitiba, PR

Jornal do Brasil Building

Rio de Janeiro, RJ

Achitect: Henrique Mindlin

Praça Dalva Simão

Belo Horizonte, MG

Praça Milton Campos

Belo Horizonte, MG

José de Alencar Theatre

Fortaleza, CE

Emir Glasner de Barros Residence

Recife, PE

Architect: Vital M.T. Pessoa de Melo

João Mauricio Nabuco Residence

Rio de Janeiro, RJ

Realdo Santos Guglielmi Residence

Criciuma, SC

1974

Pernambuco Electricity Company

Recife, PE

Architects: Reginaldo Luiz Esteves

and Vital M.T. Pessoa de Melo

**National Economic and Social
Development Bank (BNDES)**

Rio de Janeiro, RJ

Architects: Alfredo Willer, Ariel Steele, Joel Ramalho Jr,
José Sanchotene, Leonardo Oba, Rubens Sanchotene,
Oscar Müller

Indústria Textil Cía Hering

Blumenau, SC

Architect: Hans Broos

State Government House

Maceió, AL

María do Carmo Nabuco Residence

Rio de Janeiro, RJ

Mangrove Fazenda

Rio de Janeiro, RJ

Architect: Iván Gil de Mello e Souza

1975

Santa María Abbey

São Paulo, SP

Architect: Hans Broos

Manchete Building

São Paulo, SP

South Atlantic Building

Rio de Janeiro, RJ

Architects: Slomo Wenkert, Waldir Figueiredo,
Caio Rubens, Robert Fuchs and Mario Silva

Parque Laguna Rodrigo de Freitas

Rio de Janeiro, RJ

Alberto Kronsfoth Residence

Angra dos Reis, RJ

Elie Douer Residence

São Paulo, SP

Architect: Ugo di Pace

Hans Broos Residence

São Paulo, SP

Architect: Hans Broos

**João Mauricio Araujo
Pinho Residence**

Rio de Janeiro, RJ

**Brazilian Vice President's
Residence**

Brasilia, DF

Architect: Oscar Niemeyer

1976

Coronel Agostinho Promenade

Rio de Janeiro, RJ

Juan les Pins Building

Rio de Janeiro, RJ

Architects: Slomo Wenkert, Waldir Figueiredo,
Caio Rubens, Robert Fuchs and Mario Silva

Riviera di Fiori Building

Rio de Janeiro, RJ

Architects: Slomo Wenkert, Waldir Figueiredo,

Caio Rubens, Robert Fuchs and Mario Silva

World Intellectual Property Rights Organization Building

Switzerland

Architect: Pierre Braillard

National Theatre

Brasilia, DF

Architect: Oscar Niemeyer

Pithon Farias Recreational Park

Brasilia, DF

Rio Marina

Rio de Janeiro, RJ

Architect: Amaro Machado

Emilio Maya Omena Residence

Maceió, AL

Architect: Acácio Gil Borsói

Henrique Delfino Residence

Caracas, Venezuela

Architects: Siso, Shaw and Associates

João Borges de Assis

Araçatuba, SP

Architect: Clóvis Felippe Olga

Luiz Lúcio Constabile Izzo Residence

São Paulo, SP

Architect: Ruy Ohtake

Salvador J. Sequerra Residence

São Paulo, SP

Architect: Harry Cole

1977

South Bay Promenade

Florianópolis, SC

Celso de Rocha Miranda Residence

Rio de Janeiro, RJ

Edgard Hargreaves Residence

Rio de Janeiro, RJ

Architects: Roberto García Roza

and Tukie N. Brito

John Machado Urbina Residence

Caracas, Venezuela

Linneo de Paula Machado Residence

Rio de Janeiro, RJ

Architects: Otávio Moraes and Noel Marinho

1978

Galeão Airport

Rio de Janeiro, RJ

SESC Amphitheatre

Rio de Janeiro, RJ

Architects: Sérgio Jamel

and Marcos Antônio Coelho

Glaucio Carneiro Leão Residence

Recife, PE

Walter Clark Residence

Rio de Janeiro, RJ

1979

Avenida Vieira Souto Building

Rio de Janeiro, RJ

Macunaíma Building

São Paulo, SP

Architect: Marcelo Fragelli

Ministry of the Interior Building

Maceió, AL

Architect: Acácio Gil Borsói

IBM Brazil

Rio de Janeiro, RJ

Architects: José Luiz Pinho

and Glauco Campelo

Indústria Textil Cia Hering, Historical Square

Blumenau, SC

Architect: Hans Broos

**Brazilian Pavilion for Floralies
Internationales de Paris**

Paris, France

Aldo Misan Residence

Rio de Janeiro, RJ

Architect: Raphael Matheus Peres

**Aloysio Regis
Bittencourt Residence**

Rio de Janeiro, RJ

Architect: Sérgio Bernardes

Vargem Grande Fazenda

Areias, SP

Sérgio Nunes Residence

Rio de Janeiro, RJ

Architect: Guilherme Scheliga

1980

Central Bank Building

Barbados

Hering do Nordeste SA

Recife, PE

Architect: Hans Broos

Parque das Mangabeiras

Belo Horizonte, MG

Praça Tiradentes

Tiradentes, MG

Rio South Centre

Rio de Janeiro, RJ

Architects: Alexandre Cham
and Ulysses P. Burlamaqui

Barra da Tijuca Shopping Centre

Rio de Janeiro, RJ

Architect: Bernardo Figueiredo

Xerox Brazil Building

Rio de Janeiro, RJ

Architects: Pontual Associates
Architects and Planners

**Antonio Mendonça
da Silva Residence**

Uberaba, MG

Artur Falk Residence

Rio de Janeiro, RJ

Architect: Roberto García Roza
and Marcio Roberto

Denise Pontes Residence

Fortaleza, CE

Architect: Janete Ferreira da Costa

**Eduardo Pires Ferreira
Residence**

Rio de Janeiro, RJ

Architects: Eduardo Pires Ferreira

**Luiz Carlos Taques
de Mesquita Residence**

Rio de Janeiro, RJ

Architect: Sérgio Bernardes

Murilo Boabaid Residence

Rio de Janeiro, RJ

Architect: Murilo Boabaid

1981

**Boavista Bank,
Botanical Garden**

Rio de Janeiro, RJ

Architects: Pontual Associates
Architects and Planners

**Rio Business Centre:
Argentina Building and
9 de Julho Car Park**

Rio de Janeiro, RJ

Architects: Claudio Fortes
and Roberto Victor

**Rua São Francisco Xavier
Parking**

Rio de Janeiro, RJ

Largo da Carioca

Rio de Janeiro, RJ

**Antonio do Amaral
Residence**

Rio de Janeiro, RJ

Bernardez Residence

Caracas, Venezuela

Eugênio Nioac
Salles Residence

Rio de Janeiro, RJ

Fermando Mendes
Residence

Rio de Janeiro, RJ

Architect: Kátia Verbicario

Pedro Finotti
Residence

São Paulo, SP

Architect: José Guilherme Savoy de Castro

1982

Boavista Bank, Barra de Tijuca

Rio de Janeiro, RJ

Architects: Pontual Associates

Architects and Planners

Citibank Headquarters

Rio de Janeiro, RJ

Architects: Pontual Associates

Architects and Planners

Safra Bank Service Building

São Paulo, SP

Architects: Roberto Loeb

and Majer Botkowski

Barra Marina Club

Rio de Janeiro, RJ

Metalquímica de Bahía SA

Simões Filho, BA

Ministry of Education
and Culture

Rio de Janeiro, RJ

Parkshopping

Brasilia, DF

Architect: Roberto Fuchs

São Luiz Participações SA
Building

São Paulo, SP

Architect: Marcelo Fragelli

Colombo Family Residence

Rio de Janeiro, RJ

Architect: Marcelo Fragelli

Jorge Duvernoy Residence

Rio de Janeiro, RJ

Architect: Francisco Gouveia

Peter Schäefer Residence

Guarujá, SP

Architects: Alfred Talaat

and Ronaldo Racy

Raul de Sá Barbosa
Residence

Rio de Janeiro, RJ

1983

Safra Bank

Curitiba, PR

Architects: Arquiplan

Architecture and Planning

Safra Bank

Recife, PE

Architect: Sidonio Porto

Safra Bank Headquarters

São Paulo, SP

Architect: Mauricio Kogan

SESC Activity Centre,
Business Social Service,
Ilha Baião

Barra Mansa, RJ

Architects: Carlos Pini, Marcos Flaksman

and Carlos Vergara

Dallas Engineering,
Industry and Business

Campo Grande, MS

Architect: Rubens Gil de Camillo

Hotel Mar

Recife, PE

Architect: José Goiana Leal

Praça Chaim Weismann

Rio de Janeiro, RJ

Industria Textil
Vicunha Nordeste SA

Fortaleza, CE

Architect: Acácio Gil Borsói

Villa-Lobos Building

Rio de Janeiro, RJ

Elza Bebianno Residence

Rio de Janeiro, RJ

Architect: Bruno Figueiredo

Gilson Araújo Residence

Rio de Janeiro, RJ

Joseph Safra Residence

Guarujá, SP

Architect: Sérgio Bernardes

**Carabobo Fazenda
(Oscar Martinez Residence)**

Venezuela

**Raul de Souza
Martins Residence**

Petrópolis, RJ

Architect: Raul de Souza Martins

1984

Bank of Northeast Brazil

Fortaleza, CE

Architects: Marcos A. Thé Mota
and Wesson M. Nóbrega

Safra Bank Headquarters

Rio de Janeiro, RJ

Architects: Paulo Casé and
Luis Acioli Associates

**SEW de Brasil Motores,
Reductores Ltda**

Guarulhos, SP

Architects: Marcello Fragelli

Safra Bank

Belo Horizonte, MG

CAEMI Foundation

Rio de Janeiro, RJ

Architects: Edson and Edmundo Musa

**Candido Mendes
Centre Condominiums**

Rio de Janeiro, RJ

Marina Stehlin Residence

Itaipava, RJ

Santos Guglielmi Residence

Criciúma, SC

**Fernando Policarpo
de Oliveira Residence**

Niterói, RJ

Architect: Roberto Maia

H.L. Boulton Residence

Caracas, Venezuela

**José Goiana Leal
Residence**

Recife, PE

1985

Parque Laguna Maracá

Guaíra, SP

**Safra Bank,
Trianon Branch**

São Paulo, SP

Architect: Sidonio Porto

**Pan-American
Blind Factory**

Rio de Janeiro, RJ

Architect: Samuel Aratanha

Synagogue

Guarujá, SP

Architect: Mauricio Kogan

**Convent of Santo Antônio
and São Francisco**

Rio de Janeiro, RJ

Minas Rio do Norte SA

Puerto de Trombetas, Oriximiná, PA

Portal da Enseada Building

Fortaleza, CE

Eduardo Coimbra Bueno Residence

(Oca de Stockbridge)

Caçú, GO

Architect: José-Zanine Caldas

John Brenninkmeyer Residence

Cotia, SP

Architect: Robert Altman

Joseph Safra Residence

Rio de Janeiro, RJ

Moacyr Bastos Residence

Rio de Janeiro, RJ

1986

Itamaraty Annex

Brasilia, DF

Architect: Oscar Niemeyer

INCEPA –
Industria Cerámica Paraná SA

São Paulo, SP

Encol SA

Rio de Janeiro, RJ

Architect: Carlos Alberto Bittar

Jardím de Giverny Building

São Paulo, SP

Architect: Pedro Paulo Uchoa

Villa-Lobos Museum

Rio de Janeiro, RJ

Hotel Rio Poty

Teresina, PI

Architect: Ricardo Roque

Imperial Building

Rio de Janeiro, RJ

Amadeus Building

Rio de Janeiro, RJ

H. Jorge de Almeida
Chaves Residence

Itabuna

Architects: Humbert and Barbosa Andra

Evandro Ferraz Mendes
Residence

Porto Alegre, RS

Architect: Otavio Raja Gabaglia

Carlos Costa Pinto Building

Salvador, BA

Dicéa Ferraz Residence

Rio de Janeiro, RJ

Architect: Chicô Gouvêa

Eurico Villela Residence

Rio de Janeiro, RJ

Architect: Chicô Gouvêa

João José Campanillo
Ferraz Residence

Atibaiá, SP

Architect: Roberto Rondino

José Fernando Gonçalves
Féria Residence

São Paulo, SP

Tres Saltos Fazenda
(Edgard Hargreaves Residence)

Rio de Janeiro, RJ

Cristian Nacht Residence

Rio de Janeiro, RJ

1987

Coítizeiro Mineração SA Comiso

Campo Formoso, BA

Architect: Luiz Carlos Macedo

Companhia União

Rio de Janeiro, RJ

Architect: Acácio Gil Borsoi
and Janete Ferreira da Costa

Monsenhor Emilio José Salim
Ecological Park

Campinas, SP

Marco Antonio Amaral
Rezende Residence

Ilhabela, SP

Architect: Oscar Niemeyer

1988

Clóvis Rolis Ltda
Business Centre

Fortaleza, CE

Architect: Nasser Hissa Associates

Fomularios Continuos
Continac SA

Rio de Janeiro, RJ

Petrobras, Cenpes

Rio de Janeiro, RJ

Architect: Sergio Bernardez

**Cesar de Carvalho
Residence**

Petrópolis, RJ

**Pio Rodrigues Neto
Residence**

Fortaleza, CE

Architect: Luiz Fiuza

**Antonio Velasquez
Residence**

Buzios, RJ

Architect: Otavio Raja Gabaglia

Henry Lord Boulton Residence

Caracas, Venezuela

Architect: L. Zawisza

1989

Green Villa Residence

Belém, Pará, PA

**Britânia Electrodomésticos
SA Garden**

Curitiba, Paraná, PR

Architect: Vilson Cechinel Bez

West Plaza Shopping Centre

São Paulo, SP

Architects: Júlio Neves and Associates

**Norberto Geyerhahn
Residence**

Rio de Janeiro, RJ

**Vera Duvernoy
Residence**

São Paulo, SP

Architect: José Duarte Aguiar

Leo Krakowiak Residence

Ponta de Sepetuba

Ilha de São Sebastião, SP

**Mário de Castro
Residence**

Guarujá, SP

Architect: Antonio Carlos Barros Formiga

1990

Parque Jardím Chapadão

Campinas, SP

**United Nations
Business Centre**

São Paulo, SP

Architects: Botti and Rubin Associates

Aço Business Centre

São Paulo, SP

Architects: Marc Rubin and Walter Toscano

**Estação Paraiso
Metro Station**

São Paulo, SP

**Entrance Square
for the City of Cubatão**

São Paulo, SP

Mills Equipamentos Ltda

Rio de Janeiro, RJ

Torre São Paulo Building

São Paulo, SP

Architects: Ruy Ohtake, Miguel Juliano e Silva,
Ricardo Julias, Carlos Bratke, Paulo Casé,
Eduardo de Almeida, Marcos Acayaba, Roberto Loeb,
Paulo Mendes da Rocha, Eduardo Longo,
Tito Livio and Vasco de Mello

Torre Jardím Building

São Paulo, SP

Hotel Arrecifes

Jaboatão, PE

Architects: Alex Lomachinsky, Emmanuel Lins e Mello
and Mario das Gracas Correa de Araujo

Pavement for Rua 14

Volta Redonda, RJ

**Francisco Brennand
Ceramic Workshop**

Recife, PE

**Sylvia Regina Almeida
Braga Moura Residence**

Rio de Janeiro, RJ

Heinz Vollenweider Residence

Rio de Janeiro, RJ

Leo Krakowiak Residence

Ponta de Sepetuba, SP

Genipabu Seed Nursery

Salvador, BA

Avenida Presidente Vargas

Rio de Janeiro, RJ

**Cesar Augusto F.F.
Oliveira Residence**

Rio de Janeiro, RJ

**Expo 90, International Garden
and Greenery Exhibition**

Osaka, Japan

Architect: Ruy Ohtake

1991

Central Reservation of Rua 2

Volta Redonda, RJ

**João J. Campanille
Ferraz Residence**

Baoçava, SP

Architect: Roberto Rondino

Laguna Punta Porá

Paraguay

Luxembourg Gardens

Joinville, USA

**Sitio Olhos d'Agua
Development**

Ribeirão Preto, SP

**Violeta Arraes
Gervaiseau Residence**

Rio de Janeiro, RJ

Praça Saens Peña

Rio de Janeiro, RJ

**Shopping Centre,
Martão SA**

São Paulo, SP

Architect: Bernardo Figueiredo

Parque de Itaipava

Petrópolis, RJ

Architect: Glauco Campelo
and José Luiz Franca Pinho

Praça Julio de Noronha

Rio de Janeiro, RJ

Praça Harmonia

Ivoti, RS

**Parque da Praia
da Chácara**

Rio de Janeiro, RJ

**Luiz Eduardo
Ematne Residence**

Rio de Janeiro, RJ

**ABC XTAL
Microelectronics Headquarters**

Rio de Janeiro, RJ

Praça Rua Flórida

São Paulo, SP

**Hotel Avenida
Sernambetiba**

Rio de Janeiro, RJ

1992

Varginha Town Hall

Varginha, MG

Gleba D Sales Office

Barra da Tijuca, RJ

Château Roland Garros Building

Rio de Janeiro, RJ

Parque da Maré

Rio de Janeiro, RJ

Linha Vermelha (Red Line)

Rio de Janeiro, RJ

**Church of São Francisco,
Pampulha**

Belo Horizonte, MG

Morumbí Office Tower Building

São Paulo, SP

Architect: Robert Fuchs

Posto Verde

Curitiba, RJ

Praça David Ben Gurion

Laranjeiras, RJ

Otacilio Negrão de Lima Avenue and Avenue D

Belo Horizonte, MG

Perynas Islands

Cabo Frío, RJ

Architects: Gasperini Associates

Credival Building

São Paulo, SP

Architects: Julio Neves Associates

Prince of Salzburg Building

São Paulo, SP

Saint Honoré Building

São Paulo, SP

Piazza Bastione Mediceo

Pistoia, Italy

Erasmo and Irene de Falco Residence

Caracas, Venezuela

Paulista Building

São Paulo, SP

Barra Shopping

Rio de Janeiro, RJ

Eugenio and María Luiza Mendonza Residence

Rio de Janeiro, RJ

Recreio de los Bandeiratnes for Vila do Mar Residential Development

Rio de Janeiro, RJ

Hotel Beira Mar

Fortaleza, CE

Office buildings, Rua Florida

São Paulo, SP

Mural for Rua Florida

São Paulo, SP

São Marcos Real, Avenida Mendes de Moraes

Rio de Janeiro, RJ

Aterro Praia Grande

Niterói, RJ

Praça Carlos Chagas

Belo Horizonte, MG

Britador del Parque das Mangabeiras

Belo Horizonte, MG

Cidade Nova Service Station

Belo Horizonte, MG

Antonio Quinet Residence

Rio de Janeiro, RJ

Colombo Confectionery at Barra Shopping

Rio de Janeiro, RJ

Joseph Safra Residence

Morumbí, SP

Copacabana Palace

Rio de Janeiro, RJ

Marambaia Fazenda, football pitch and adjoining facilities

Rio de Janeiro, RJ

Country Village Condominium Entrance

Ribeirão Preto, SP

Central Reservation of Rua General Glicério

Laranjeiras, RJ

Biscayne Boulevard

Miami, Florida, USA

1993

Jorge Zahran Residence

Campo Grande, MS

Rosa Luxembourg Platz

Berlin, Germany

Pactual Bank

Rio de Janeiro, RJ

Praça Avenida das Américas

Guarujá, SP

Kupfer Residence

Guarujá, SP

Architect: Marco Acayaba

Cascata Fazenda

Araras, SP

Camburn Residence

Barra de Guaratiba, RJ

Le Premier Residential Building

Porto Alegre, RGS

Paragem da Cantaria Condominiums

Ouro Preto, MG

Jardím das Perdizes Residential Building

São Paulo, SP

Rogério and Maria Célia de Araujo Residence

Rio de Janeiro, RJ

Parque Ibirapuera Sculpture Garden

São Paulo, SP

Kuala Lumpur City Central Park

Kuala Lumpur, Malaysia

Machado Residence

Laranjeiras, RJ

Mussi Toledo Museum

Minas Gerais, MG

Andreas Klein Residence

Ilha Grande, Angra dos Reis, RJ

Supreme Court of the State of Rio de Janeiro

Rio de Janeiro, RJ

VIP Lounge, Safra Bank

Guarulhos International Airport, São Paulo

Sulamita and Saul Mareines Residence

Rio de Janeiro, RJ

Museum of Modern Art

Rio de Janeiro, RJ

Rio II Sul

Rio de Janeiro, RJ

Marco A.A. Resende Residence

São Paulo, SP

1994

Music Centre

São Conrado, RJ

Colina

São Francisco, RJ

Teleporto

Rio de Janeiro, RJ

Castaldi Residence

São Paulo, SP

Roberto Burle Marx Palm Garden Exhibition

Frankfurt, Germany

Sulamita Mareines Residence, Tree of Life Garden

Israel

Rio Claro Shopping Centre

São Paulo, SP

Residential Building on Avenida Beira Mar

Fortaleza, CE

Fortaleza Botanical Gardens

Fortaleza, CE

Awards and Honours

1941

Gold Medal for Painting,
National School of Fine Art
Rio de Janeiro

1953

Prize, First International Architecture
Exhibition, II São Paulo Biennial
São Paulo

1954

Gold Medal for Painting,
XLVII Fine Arts Salon
Rio de Janeiro

1957

Prize,
Floralies Internationales de Paris
Paris

1958

Prize for the gardens of the Brazilian
Pavilion, Brussels International Fair
Brussels

1959

Knight of the Order of the Crown
Belgium

1960

Gold Medal, International Flower Show
Trieste, Italy

Commemorative medal for the
inauguration of the Monument to
the Fallen of World War II
Rio de Janeiro

Honorary Member of the National Society
of Interior Designers
USA

1962

Commander of the Order of Merit
Santiago, Chile

1963

First Prize, First Jewellery Exhibition, VII
São Paulo Biennial
São Paulo

Bronze Medal, IGA 63,
International Garden Exhibition
Hamburg, Germany

Santos Dumont Medal of Merit
Brazil

Gold Medal,
International Flower Show
Trieste, Italy

1964

Silver Medal,
Floralies Internationales de Paris
Paris

1965

Prize, Fine Arts Medal,
American Institute of Architects
Washington DC, USA

First Prize for Jewellery, I Uruguayan
Applied Arts Biennial
Montevideo, Uruguay

Participation in the Brazilian Federal
Council of Culture
Rio de Janeiro

Honorary Member of the British Columbia
Society of Landscape Architects
Vancouver, Canada

1969

Honorary Member of the Florida
Association of Landscape Architects
Florida, USA

Personality of the Year, Rio Institute of
Brazilian Architects
Rio de Janeiro

Medal from the SENAC School,
Copacabana
Rio de Janeiro

1970
Commander of the Order of Merit,
Centenary Order
Nicaragua

Estácio de Sá Trophy, Museum
of Image and Sound
Rio de Janeiro

1971
Decoration, Order of Rio Branco
Itamaraty, Brazil

Diploma and Honorary Member,
Campo Grande Institute of Culture
Rio de Janeiro

1972
Member of the Guanabara
Urban Planning Council,
Government of the State of Rio
Rio de Janeiro

Guest of Honour,
Ecuadorean College of Architects
Quito, Ecuador

1973
Honorary Member, Pernambuco Institute
of Brazilian Architects
Pernambuco, Brazil

1974
Honorary Member, Rio Grande
do Sul Association for the Protection
of the Environment
Rio Grande do Sul, Brazil

APCA Prize, São Paulo Art Critics
Association
São Paulo

Caixas do Sul Medal, Municipality
of Caixas do Sul
Rio Grande do Sul, Brazil

1975
Martim Afonso de Sousa
Cultural Medal, Guarujá Historical
and Geographical Institute
Bertioga, São Paulo

1976
Honra da Inconfidência Medal
Belo Horizonte, Brazil

Honorary Member No. 1, Brazilian
Association of Landscape Architects
São Paulo

1977
Decoration, Republic of Venezuela
Venezuela

Prize, American Institute
of Landscape Architects
USA

1978
Roquete Pinto Trophy, TV Record
São Paulo

1979
Honorary Member, American Academy
and Institute of Arts and Letters
New York, USA

Gran Medalla de Inconfidência
Belo Horizonte, Brazil

Participation in the Rio Botanical Gardens
Consultative Council
Rio de Janeiro

Honorary Member of Paraíba Friends
of Nature Association
Paraíba, Brazil

1981

Member of the Bavarian Academy
of Fine Arts
Bavaria, Germany

Grand Officer of the Order of
Arts and Letters, Ministry of Culture
and Communication
France

1982

Gold Medal,
Academy of Architecture
Paris

Doctor Honoris Causa,
Royal College of Art
London

Doctor Honoris Causa,
Royal Academy of Fine Arts
The Hague, Netherlands

1983

Honorary Member,
Brazilian Botanical Society
Brazil
Bull Brazil Prize, V Maldonado Biennial
Maldonado, Uruguay

Albert P. and Blanche V. Greensfelder
Award, Missouri Botanical Gardens
Missouri, USA

1985

Oliveira Lima Cultural Merit Medal,
Government of the State
of Pernambuco
Pernambuco, Brazil

Grand Cross of the Order
of Merit, Government of
the Federal District
Brasilia, Brazil

ASLA Medal, American Society of
Landscape Architecture
Cincinatti, USA

Colonel of Kentucky, Honorary Citizen of
Louisville and Member of the Kentucky
Botanical Gardens
Kentucky, USA

Bremmer Ehrler, High Court Judge of
Jefferson County, Kentucky, proclaims
4 October 1985 Burle Marx Day
Jefferson Country, USA

1987

Commander of the Order of Merit,
Government of the State of Mato Grosso
Mato Grosso, Brazil

Mérito Alvorada Medal,
Government of the Federal District
Brasilia, Brazil

1988

Pedro Ernesto Medal, Rio de Janeiro
Municipal Chamber
Rio de Janeiro

Doctor Honoris Causa, Rio de Janeiro
State University
Rio de Janeiro

1989

Honorary Member, Canadian Society of
Landscape Architects
Canada

National Library Medal
Rio de Janeiro

Roberto Burle Marx Prize created
for the Second Monographic Competition
of the Third Age Foundation, on the
theme 'Old Age in Brazil – New Ways'

1990

Doctor Honoris Causa, Rio de Janeiro
Federal University
Rio de Janeiro

First Carlo Scarpo International Garden
Prize, Benetton Foundation
Treviso, Italy

Honorary Citizen, Municipality
of Vila de Constância
Constância, Portugal

Diploma for Contribution to the
Development and Culture
of the City of Rio de Janeiro
Rio de Janeiro

Tribute from the University of Santa
Ursula, Second Botanical Seminar
Rio de Janeiro

Order of Cultural Merit,
Government of the Federal District
Brasilia, Brazil

1991
First Prize (IAB-RJ), Competition for
preliminary study for Parque de Itaipava
Petrópolis, Brazil

1992
Honorary Citizen, Municipality of Belo
Horizonte
Belo Horizonte, Brazil

Leonardo da Vinci Prize, World Award
for Arts 1991, Rio de Janeiro
State University
Rio de Janeiro

Honorary Citizen, Federal District
Legislative Chamber
Brasilia, Brazil

Tribute from the Minister of Culture and
Brazilian Visual Arts Association for
International Art Connection – Eco 1992
Rio de Janeiro

Doctor Honoris Causa, Florence University
Faculty of Architecture
Florence, Italy

Honorary Citizen
Pistoia, Italy

Honorary Member of the Italian National
Association of Directors of Parks and
Public Gardens
Pistoia, Italy

1993
Honorary Citizen, Municipality of Rio de
Janeiro
Rio de Janeiro

1994
Grand Officer of the Order of Rio Branco
Brasilia, Brazil

Bibliography

Adams, William Howard, *Roberto Burle Marx: The Unnatural Art of the Garden* (New York, Museum of Modern Art, 1991).

Architecture d'Aujourd'hui, August 1952, October 1953 and November 1972 issues. (Paris, France)

Bardi, Pietro María, *The Tropical Gardens of Burle Marx* (Rio de Janeiro, Colibris Editora Ltda, 1964).

Benoist-Méchin , J., *L'homme et ses jardins* (*Man and his Gardens*) (Paris, Albin/Michel, 1975).

Burle Marx, Roberto, *Arte e Paisagem* (*Art and Landscape*), selected conferences (São Paulo, Editorial Nobel, 1987).

Burle Marx, Roberto; Ono, Haruyoshi and Tabacow, José, *Plantas bem brasileiras presentadas por Burle Marx* (*The Plants of Brazil Presented by Burle Marx*) (Rio de Janeiro, Rio Editora, 1980).

Cals, Soraia, *Roberto Burle Marx: uma fotobiografia* (*Roberto Burle Marx: a Photobiography*) (Rio de Janeiro, Banco Cidam, 1995).

Coelho Frota, Lélia, *Burle Marx: Paisagismo no Brasil* (*Burle Marx: Landscape Design in Brazil*) (São Paulo, Câmara Brasileira do Livro, 1994).

Coelho Frota, Lélia; de Hollanda, Gastão; Leenhardt, Jacques and Kruger, Bernd, *Burle Marx, uma poética da modernidade* (*Burle Marx, Poetry of Modernity*) (Minas Gerais, Compoart Ed., 1989).

Costa, Lúcio, *Burle Marx, homenagem a natureza* (*Burle Marx: Homage to Nature*) (São Paulo, Editorial Vozes, 1979).

Costa, Lúcio, *Registro de una vivencia* (São Paulo, Empresa das Artes, 1995)

Cousin, Jean-Pierre, 'Brésil' in *Architecture d'Aujourd'hui* no. 251, June 1987, Brazil issue.

Delacampagne, Christian, *La Peinture Moderne* (Edition Menges, 1988).

Eliovsen, Sima, *The Gardens of Roberto Burle Marx* (Oregon, Sagapress/Timber Press and London, Thames & Hudson,1991).

Ferraz, Geraldo and Valladares, Clarival, Catalogue of Rio de Janeiro Museum of Modern Art (Rio de Janeiro, 1963).

Fleming, Lawrence, *Roberto Burle Marx, um retrato* (Rio de Janeiro, Editora Index, 1996); *A Portrait of Robert Burle Marx* (Art Books International, 1996)

Gonçalves, Lisbeth Rebollo, *Arte e Paisagem: a Estetica de Roberto Burle Marx* (*Art and Landscape: The Aesthetic of Roberto Burle Marx*) (São Paulo, MAC-USP, 1997).

Hamerman, Conrad, 'Roberto Burle Marx: the Last Interview' in *The Journal of Decorative and Propaganda Arts*, 1995 (USA) Brazil issue.

Hitchcock, Henry Russell, *Latin American Architecture since 1945* (New York, Museum of Modern Art, 1955).

Kassler, Elizabeth B., *Modern Gardens and the Landscape* (New York, Museum of Modern Art, 1964/1984).

Leenhardt, Jacques, *Dans les jardins de Roberto Burle Marx* (*In the Gardens of Roberto Burle Marx*) (Arles, Actes Sud/Crestet, 1994).

Mazza Dourado, G. et al, *Visões de Paisagem* (*Visions of Landscape*) (São Paulo, Brazilian Association of Landscape Architects, 1997).

Mosser, Monique, 'Jardins et peinture' ('Gardens and Painting') in *Actualité des arts plastiques* no. 62, 1984, Centre National de documentation pédagogique (Paris, France).

Motta, Flávio L., *Roberto Burle Marx e a nova visão da paisagem* (*Roberto Burle Marx and the New Vision of Landscape*) (São Paulo, Editorial Nobel, 1984).

Monuments Historiques no. 143, February/March 1986 (France).

Niemeyer, Oscar, *Rio* (Rio de Janeiro, Avenir Editora, 1980).

Nuestra Arquitectura no. 26, August 1955 (Argentina).

Paul, Anthony and Rees, Yvonne, *The Garden Design Book* (London, William Collins Sons, 1988).

Rizzo, Giulio G., *Il giardino del Novecento* (*The Nineteeth-Century Garden*) (Florence, Camini, 1992).

Ross, S., *What Gardens Mean* (Chicago, University of Chicago Press, 1998).

Rykwert, Joseph, *Rassegna* no. 8, October 1981, pp. 5-12 (Italy).

Schinz, Marina, *O mundo dos jardins* (*The World of Gardens*) (Rio de Janeiro, Editorial Salamandra, 1985).

Schwob, Daniel Colson, 'Brésil' in *Techniques et Architecture* no. 334, March 1981 (France).

Soares, Silvio Macedo, *Quadro do Paisagismo no Brasil* (*Landscape Design in Brazil*) (São Paulo, Gráfica Pancrom, 1999).

Summa, December 1963 and December 1965 issues (Argentina).

Valladares, Clarival, *A unidade plastica na obra de Burle Marx* (*Visual Unity in the Work of Burle Marx*) (Rio de Janeiro, Cadernos Brasileiros, 1965).

Valladares, Clarival, *43 anos de pintura: Roberto Burle Marx* (*43 Years of Painting: Roberto Burle Marx*) (Belo Horizonte Museum, 1972).

Vaccarino, Rossana (ed.), *Roberto Burle Marx: Landscapes Reflected* (New York, Princeton Architectural Press, 2000).

Willet, John, *Les années Weimar* (*The Weimar Years*) (Paris, F. Hazan, 1984).

Williams, Amancio, Catálogo del Museo Nacional de Bellas Artes (Buenos Aires, 1961).

Zevi, Bruno, 'Paesagistica brasiliana: I giardini compensatori', *Cronache de architetettura* vol II, no. 162, 1970 (Italy, Edizione La Terza).

Zevi, Bruno, Catalogue of the Fifth São Paulo Biennial, 1959.

Zevi, Bruno, *Historia de la Arquitectura Moderna* (Barcelona, Ed. Poseidon, 1980), p. 386-7.

Picture Credits

Index